The Complete Guitar Player
Rock Songbook

Published by:
Wise Publications
14-15 Berners Street, London W1T 3LJ, UK.

Exclusive Distributors:
Music Sales Limited
Distribution Centre, Newmarket Road, Bury St Edmunds, Suffolk IP33 3YB, UK.
Music Sales Corporation
180 Madison Avenue, 24th Floor, New York NY 10016, USA.
Music Sales Pty Limited
Units 3-4, 17 Willfox Street, Condell Park, NSW 2200, Australia.

Compiled and edited by Toby Knowles.
Music processed by shedwork.com.
Cover designed by Fresh Lemon.
Printed in the EU.

The Complete Guitar Player
Rock Songbook

Wise Publications
part of The Music Sales Group
London / New York / Paris / Sydney / Copenhagen / Berlin / Madrid / Hong Kong / Tokyo

All Day And All Of The Night

Words & Music by Ray Davies

> The strumming rhythm shown in the intro should be played with solid, detached down-strums. Play it in the verse, too, before a freer feel for the chorus.

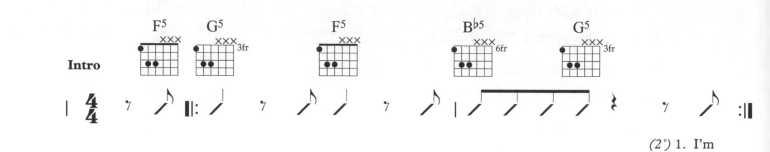

Intro

(2°) 1. I'm

Verse

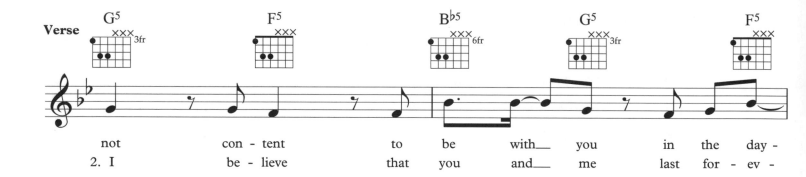

not con-tent to be with__ you in the day-
2. I be-lieve that you and__ me last for-ev-

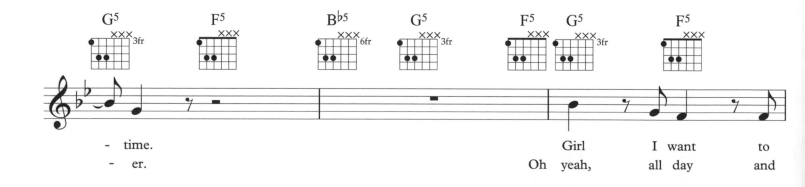

- time.   Girl   I want   to
- er.   Oh yeah,   all day   and

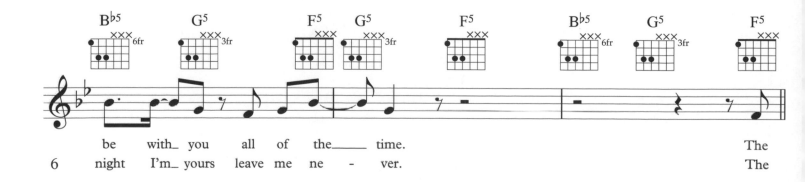

be with__ you all of the___ time.   The
6 night I'm__ yours leave me ne - ver.   The

Chorus

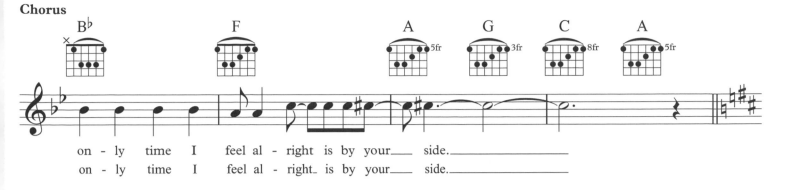

on - ly time I feel al - right is by your___ side.___
on - ly time I feel al - right_ is by your___ side.___

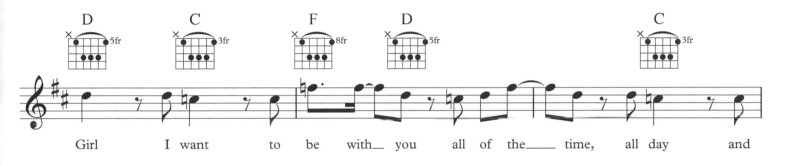

Girl I want to be with__ you all of the___ time, all day and

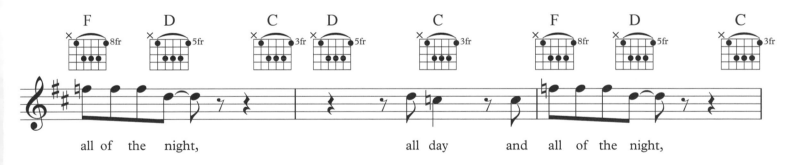

all of the night, all day and all of the night,

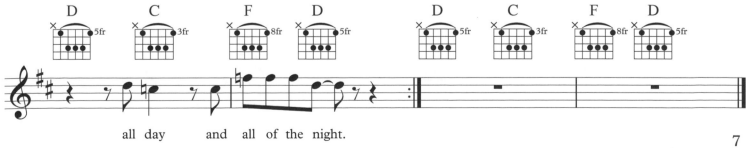

all day and all of the night.

All Right Now

Words & Music by Paul Rodgers & Andy Fraser

Strumming style:

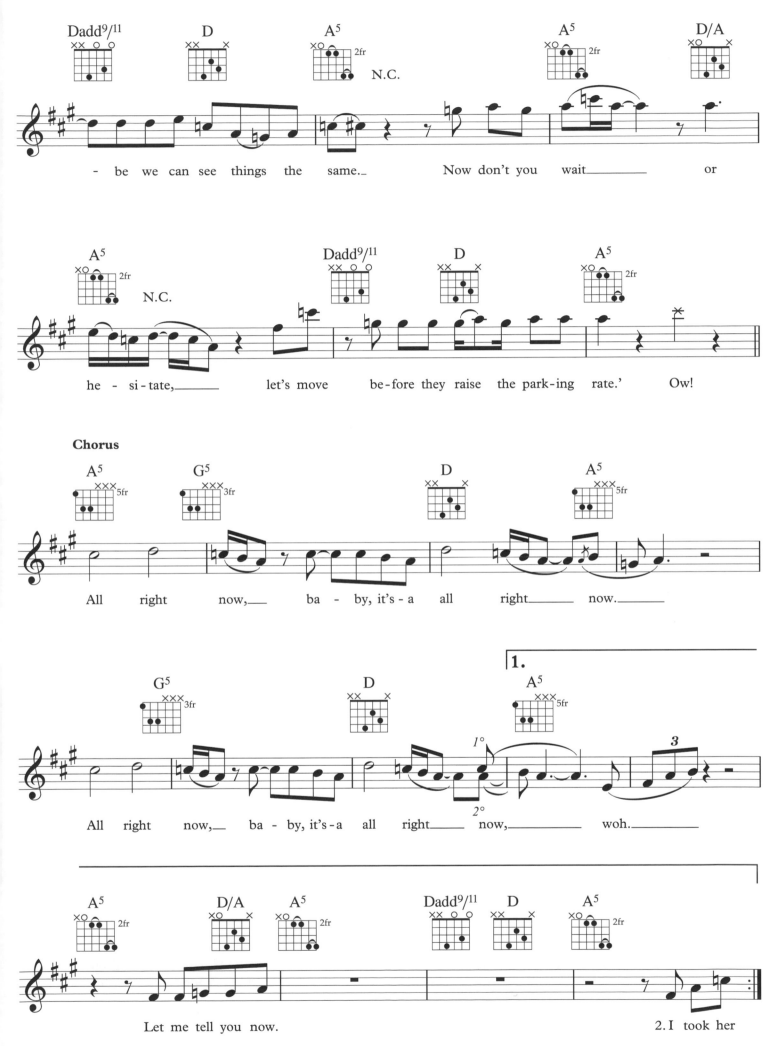

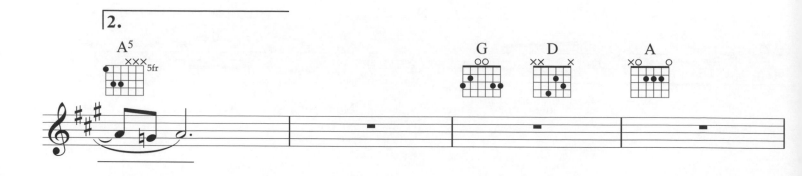

Guitar Solo

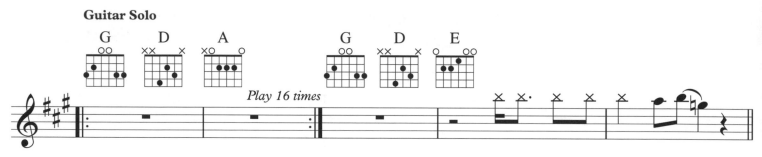

Play 16 times

I said, don't you know. Oh, yeah.

Outro

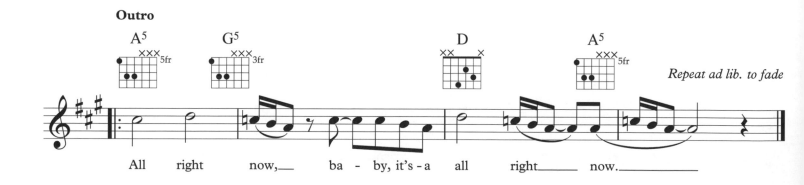

Repeat ad lib. to fade

All   right   now,___   ba - by, it's - a   all   right___   now.___

Verse 2:
I took her home to my place,
Watchin' every move on her face.
She said 'Look, what's your game, baby?
Are you try'n' to put me in shame?'

I said-a, 'Slow, don't go so fast,
Don't you think that love can last?'
She said, 'Love, Lord above,
Now you're try'n' to trick me in love.'

Alone

Words & Music by Tom Kelly & Billy Steinberg

Picking style:

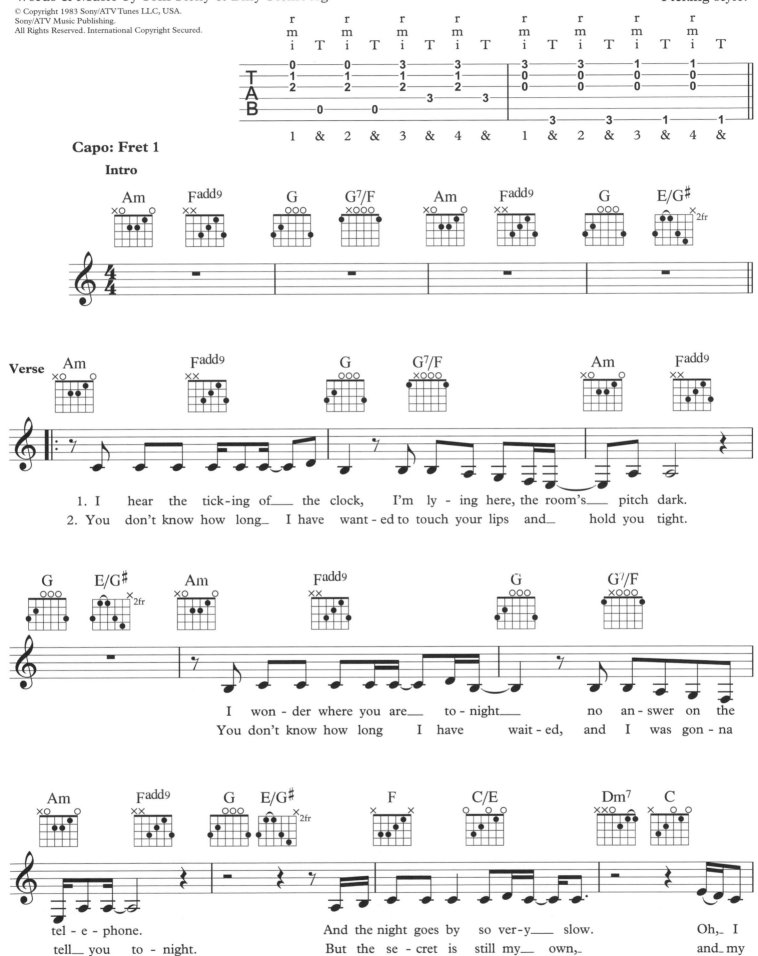

Capo: Fret 1

Intro

Verse

1. I hear the tick-ing of___ the clock, I'm ly - ing here, the room's___ pitch dark.
2. You don't know how long_ I have want - ed to touch your lips and_ hold you tight.

I won - der where you are___ to - night___ no an - swer on the
You don't know how long I have wait - ed, and I was gon - na

tel - e - phone.
tell_ you to - night.

And the night goes by so ver-y___ slow.
But the se - cret is still my_ own,_

Oh,_ I
and_ my

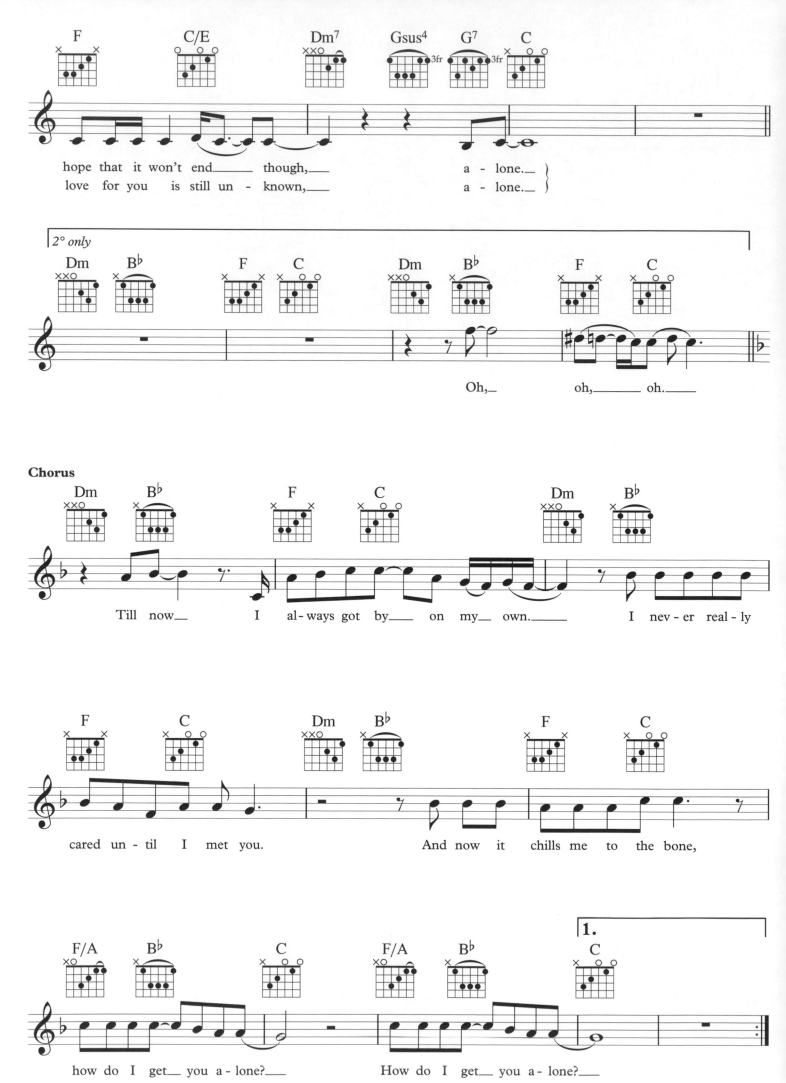

hope that it won't end_____ though,_____
love for you is still un - known,_____

a - lone.__
a - lone.__

2° only

Oh,__ oh,_____ oh._____

Chorus

Till now__ I al-ways got by__ on my__ own._____ I nev - er real - ly

cared un - til I met you. And now it chills me to the bone,

1.

how do I get__ you a - lone?____ How do I get__ you a - lone?____

Oh, oh.

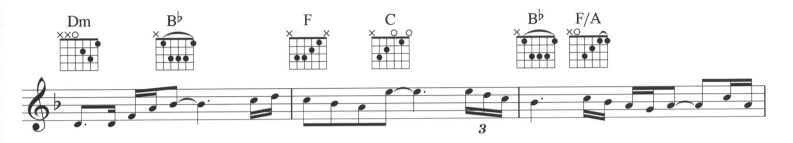

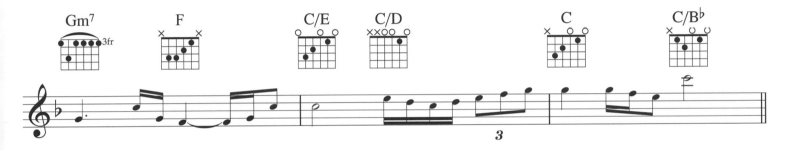

Outro Chorus

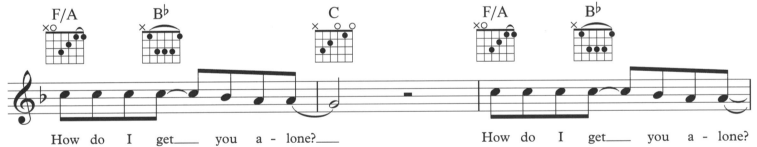

How do I get you a - lone? How do I get you a - lone?

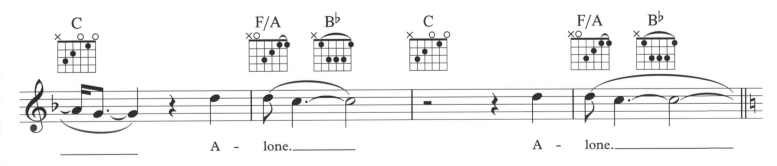

A - lone. A - lone.

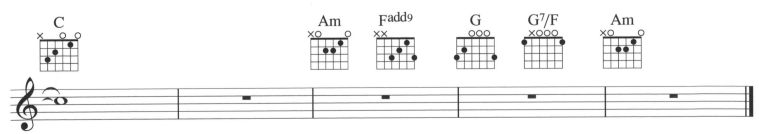

Crazy Little Thing Called Love

Words & Music by Freddie Mercury

(like a ba - by) in a cra - dle all night,_ it swings_ (woo woo) it jives_

_ (woo woo) it shakes all o - ver like a jel - ly - fish__ I kind - a

like it Cra - zy lit - tle thing called love.__ There goes my

Bridge

ba - by,_____ she knows how to rock and roll._ She drives me

cra - zy_____ she gives me hot and cold fe - ver, then she leaves me in a cool, cool sweat.

(Guitar/Bass)

I got - ta be cool_

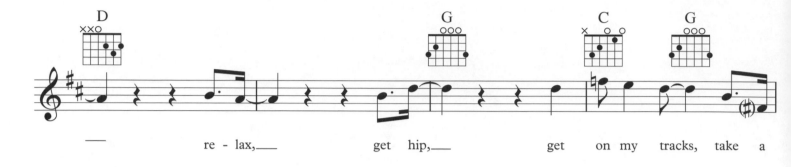

— re - lax,___ get hip,___ get on my tracks, take a

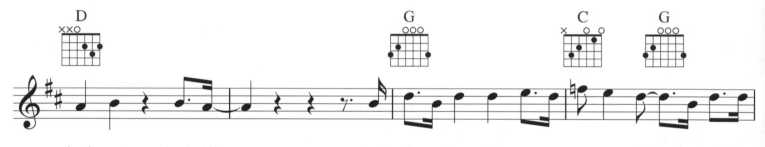

back seat, hitch-hike,___ And take a long ride on my mot-or - bike_ un-til I'm

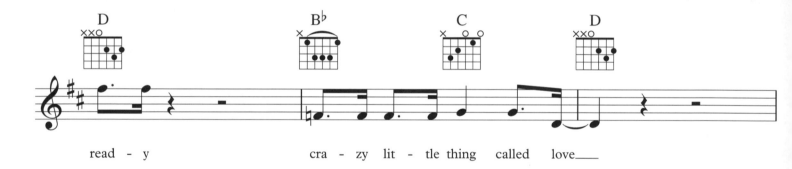

read - y cra - zy lit - tle thing called love___

Guitar Solo

N.C.

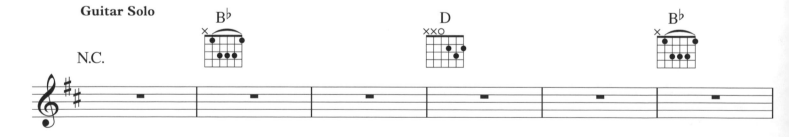

N.C. *(Guitar/Bass)*

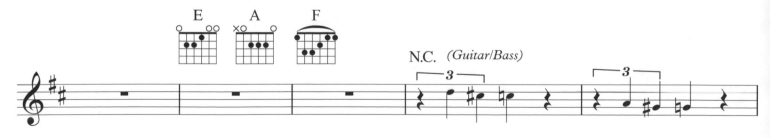

Born To Be Wild

Words & Music by Mars Bonfire

fire all of your guns___ at once_ and ex-plode in-to space,_____

Chorus

_____ Like a true na-ture's child_____ we were born, born to be wild_

__ we can climb so high_ I ne-ver want to die._____

Born to be wild,_____

Born to be wild._____

Instrumental Solo

Repeat 5 times ad lib. **Drum Solo**
(%) Repeat to fade

D.S.

Call Me

Words by Deborah Harry
Music by Giorgio Moroder

Strumming style:

Dm G5 F5 Dm F5 C5

1 & 2 & 3 & 4 & 1 & 2 & 3 & 4 & 1 & 2 & 3 & 4 & 1 & 2 & 3 & 4 &

Intro (Drums)

Dm G5 F5 Dm F5 C5

Verse

Dm   B♭

1. Col-our me___ your col-our, ba-by; col-our me___ your car.___
2. Cov-er me___ with kiss-es, ba-by; cov-er me___ with love.___

Dm   B♭

Col-our me___ your col-our, dar-ling; I know who___ you are.___
Roll me in___ de-sign-er sheets, I'll___ nev-er get e-nough.___ E-

Gm A Gm A7

1° only

Come up off___ your col-our chart, I know where you're com-ing from.___ Call me,___
- mo-tions come,___ I don't___ know why, cov-er up___ love's

20

2° *only*

A⁷   Dm   F

al - i - bi.   — on the line;   call me,
        Call me,   on the line;   call me,

Gm   B♭   Dm   F

call me an - y, an - y - time. Call me,   my love;   you can
call me an - y, an - y - time. Call me,   oh, my love;   when you're

Gm   B♭   Dm   G⁵   F⁵

call me an - y day   or night. Call me!
read - y we can share the wine. Call me!

1.   **2.**

Dm   F⁵   C⁵   Em⁷   Am   G

Bridge

Em   Bm⁷

Ooh,   he speaks the lan - gua - ges   of love.

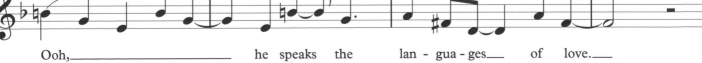

21

Ooh,_____ a - mo - re chi - a - ma - mi,____ chia-ma-mi.

Ooh,_____ ap - pelle - moi mon che - rie____ ap-pelle - moi. An - y - time,___

____ an - y place, an - y - where,____ an - y - way._____ An - y - time,___

____ an - y place,_ an - y-where,____ an - y - day._____

Instrumental

22

Call me,

Chorus

my love;__ call me, call me an-y, an-y-time.__ Call

me, for a ride;__ call me, call me for some o-ver-time.__ Call

me, my love;__ call me, call me in a sweet de-sign.__ Call

me, call me for your lov-er's lov-er's al-i-bi.__ Call

me on the line,__ call me, call me an-y, an-y-time.__ Call

Repeat and fade

me! Oh, call me, ooh,__ ooh,__ ah.__ Call

23

Chasing Cars

Words & Music by Paul Wilson, Gary Lightbody, Jonathan Quinn, Nathan Connolly & Tom Simpson

Chorus

here,   if I just lay   here,   would you lie

with   me   and   just for - get the world?

For - get what we're   told

be - fore we get   too   old.   Show me a

gar - den that's burst-ing in - to life.

Verse

3. Let's waste time   chas - ing cars

a - round   our heads.

25

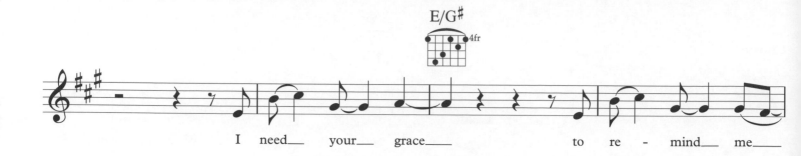

I need___ your___ grace___ to re - mind___ me___

___ to find___ my___ own.___ If I lay

Chorus

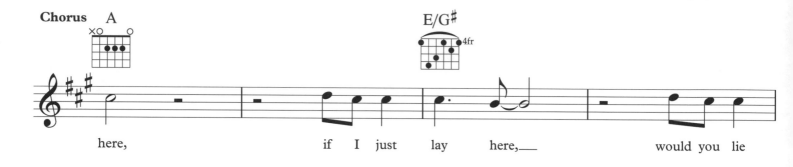

here, if I just lay here,___ would you lie

with me___ and___ just for - get the world?___ For-get what we're

told___ be-fore we get too old.___ Show me a

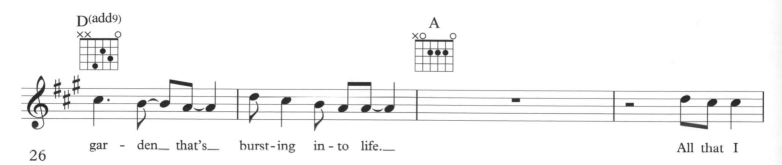

gar - den___ that's___ burst-ing in-to life.___ All that I

26

Cocaine

Words & Music by J.J. Cale

This entire song can be played with a single barred shape using just one finger! It's how J.J. Cale played it himself. Add a little crunchy overdrive, and you're good to go!

Intro

(Guitar rhythm sim.)

1. If you

Verse

wan - na hang out, you got to take her out;— co-caine.—
(2.) got bad— news, you wan-na kick them blues; co-caine.—
(3.) thing— is gone and you wan-na ride on; co-caine.—

If you wan - na get down, down on the ground; co - caine.—
When your day is— done and you wan - na run; co - caine.—
Don't for - get this— fact: you can't get— back; co - caine.—

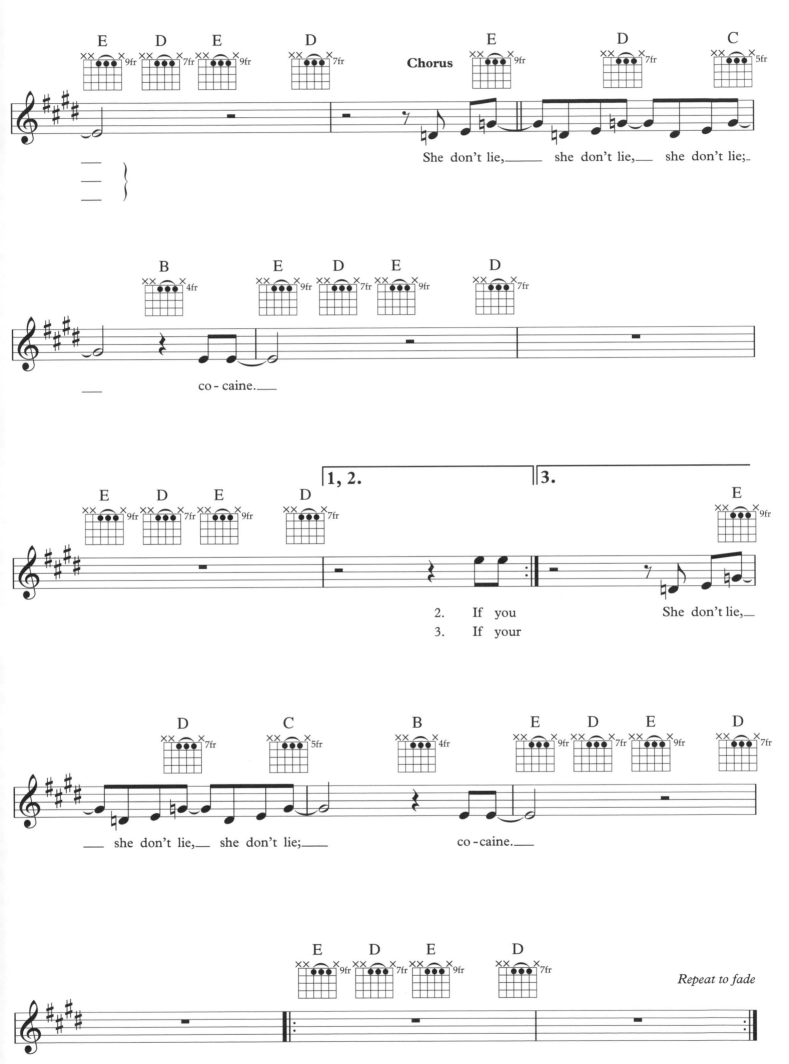

Black

Words by Eddie Vedder
Music by Stone Gossard

It's enough to play a single chord per bar for this song, allowing it to ring on. Create a dense, dark sound with distortion and a little reverb. For the chorus, try constant eighth-note down-strums.

1. Sheets of emp-ty can - vas,___ un-touched sheets of clay___ were

laid spread out be-fore___ me___ as her___ bo-dy once did.___ 2. Oh,

all___ five ho-ri - zons re-volved___ a - round her soul___ as the earth to the sun.
3. I take a walk___ out - side,___ I'm___sur-roun-ded by___ some kids___ at___ play.

Now the air I tas - ted and breathed has___ ta-ken a turn.___ Ooh,___
I can feel their laugh - ter,___ so why do I sear? Ooh,___

Chorus

oh, and all I_ taught_ her was_ eve - ry thing._
oh, and twis- ted_ thoughts_ that spin_ round my head,_ I'm spin- ning,

Oh,_____ I know she_ gave_ me all_ that she_
oh._ I'm spinning, how quick the_ sun_ can drop a -

_ wore._ And now my_ bit-ter_ hands chafe be - neath_
- way._ And now my_ bit-ter_ hands cra - dle_ bro -

_ the clouds of_ what was eve - ry thing._ Oh, the pic - tures_
- ken glass_ of_ what was eve - ry thing._

1.
_ have all been_ washed_ in black, tat-tooed eve-ry thing._

2.
_____ All the love_gone bad turned my_world_ to black, tat-tooed all I_ see,_ all that_ I_

___ am,__ all I'll be,___

I

Outro

know some-day you'll have a beau-ti-ful life.__ I know you'll be a star__ in some-

-bo-dy else-'s sky.__ But why,__ why,__ why_____ can't it be,_

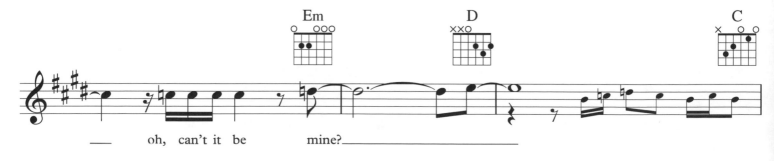

__ oh, can't it be mine?_____

Repeat to fade

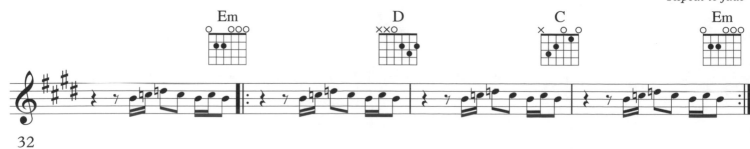

Creep

Words & Music by Albert Hammond, Mike Hazlewood, Thom Yorke,
Jonny Greenwood, Colin Greenwood, Ed O'Brien & Phil Selway

Picking pattern:

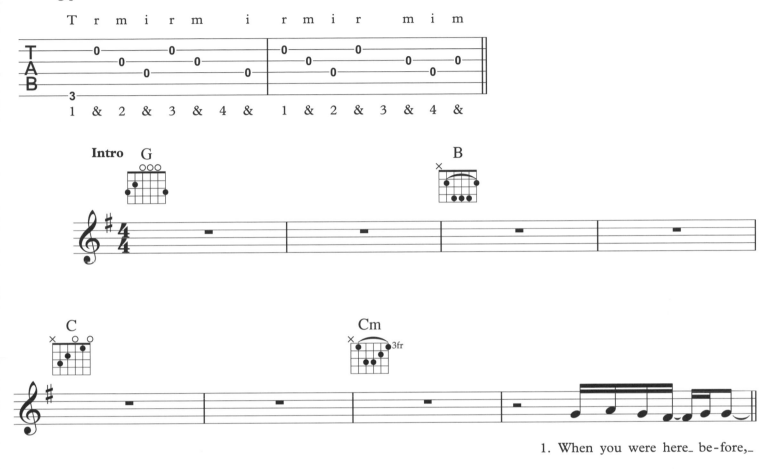

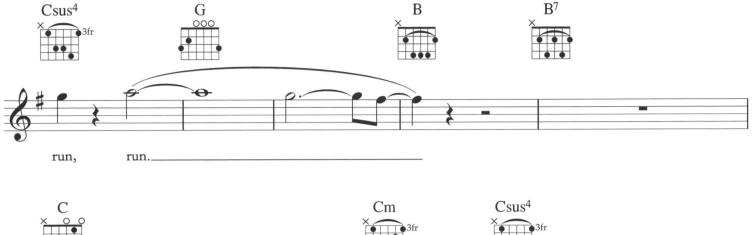

run,   run._____

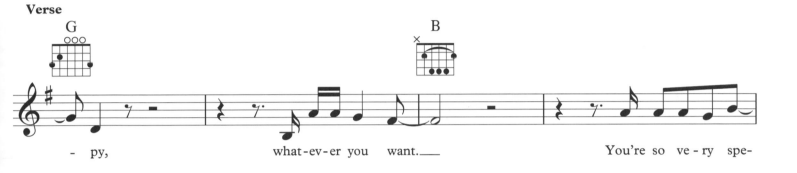

Run._____ 3. What-ev-er makes you hap-

Verse

- py,   what-ev-er you want.____ You're so ve-ry spe_

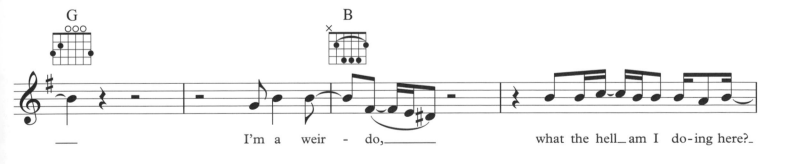

- cial,   I wish I was spe - cial.   But I'm a creep,__

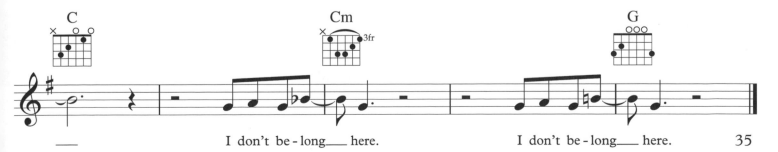

___   I'm a weir - do,_____   what the hell__ am I do-ing here?_

___   I don't be-long___ here.   I don't be-long___ here.

Don't Look Back In Anger

Words & Music by Noel Gallagher

So I start a re-vo-lu-tion from my bed, 'cause you

said the brains I had went to my head. Step out-side, sum-mer-time's in

bloom, stand up be-side the fire - place, take that look from off your face,

you ain't ev-er gon - na burn my heart out. And

Chorus

so Sal - ly can wait, she knows it's too late as we're walk - ing on by.

Her soul slides a - way,___ but 'Don't_ look back_

___ in an - ger', I heard you say.___ (Gtr.)

Guitar Solo

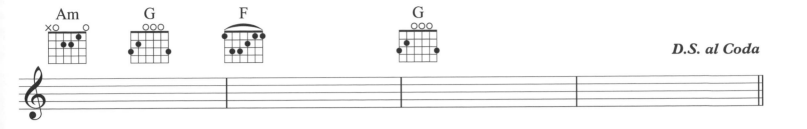

D.S. al Coda

So Sal - ly can wait,___ she knows it's too late___

___ as she's walk - ing on by._____ Her soul slides a - way,___

___ but 'Don't___ look back___ in an - ger, don't look back in an - ger',___

___ I heard you say.___ At least not to - day.

Eye Of The Tiger

Words & Music by Jim Peterik & Frank Sullivan III

A second guitar can play the constant sixteenth-notes shown below throughout the intro and verses. Aim for a detached, steady pulse to accompany the main rhythm part.

man and his will   to sur-vive.___   So man-y times   it hap-pens too fast,

You trade your pas-sion for glo - ry.___   Don't lose your grip_   on the

dreams of   the   past, You must fight   just   to keep   them a - live___   It's___   the

Chorus

eye of the tig - er, it's the thrill of the fight,   ris - ing   up   to the chal-lenge of our

To Coda ⊕

riv - al.   And___   the   last known sur-vi - vor stalks his   prey in the night,   and___ he's

1.

watch-ing us   all with the   eye_____   of   the tig - er.

41

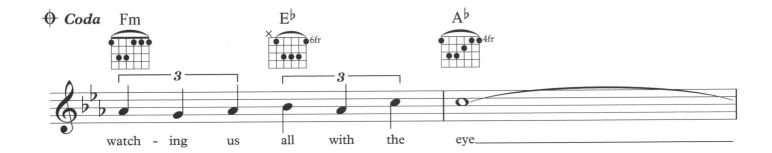

watch - ing   us   all   with   the   eye_____

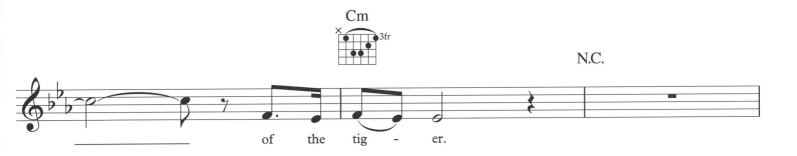

_____   of   the   tig - er.

Outro

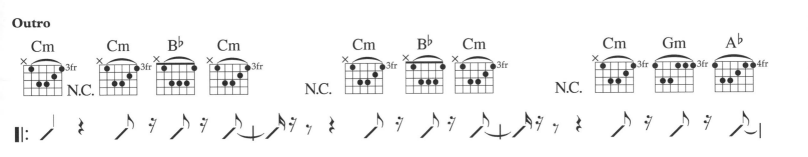

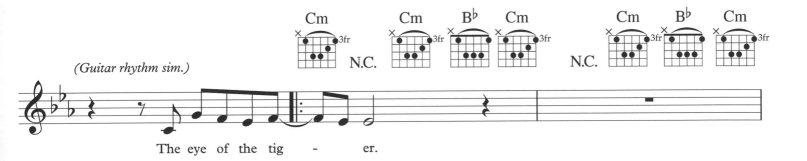

(Guitar rhythm sim.)

The   eye   of   the   tig   -   er.

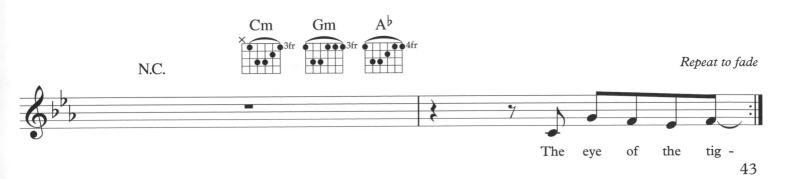

Repeat to fade

The   eye   of   the   tig -

43

Every Breath You Take

Words & Music by Sting

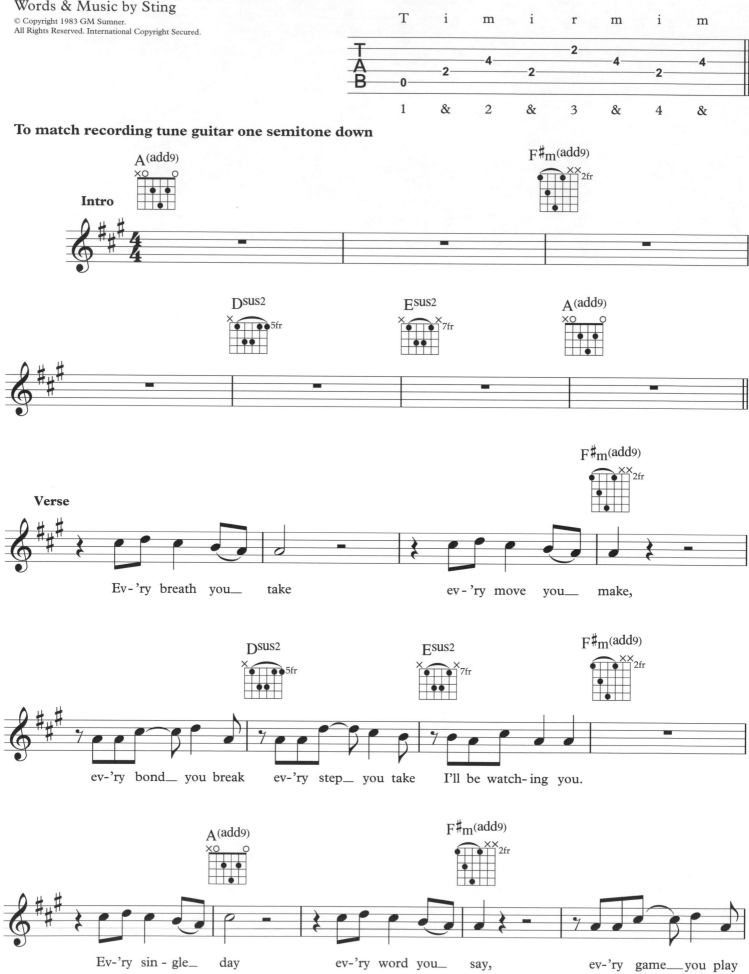

To match recording tune guitar one semitone down

Ev-'ry breath you___ take   ev-'ry move you___ make,

ev-'ry bond___ you break   ev-'ry step___ you take   I'll be watch-ing you.

Ev-'ry sin-gle___ day   ev-'ry word you___ say,   ev-'ry game___ you play

ev-'ry night___ you stay, I'll be watch-ing you.

Oh, can't you___

Chorus

see you be- long to me.

How my poor heart___

___ aches___ with ev-'ry step___ you take.

Ev-'ry move you___

make ev-'ry vow you___ break,

ev-'ry smile you fake

To Coda ⊕

ev-'ry claim you stake, I'll be watch-ing you.

Since you've gone,___ I been lost___ with - out___ a trace,

I dream at night I can on-

F

- ly see__ your face, I look a-round but it's you I can't__ re-place, I feel so cold and I

F

long for your__ em- brace. I keep cry - ing ba - by ba - by please.__

A(add9)   **F#m**(add9)   **D**sus2

Esus2   **A**(add9)

D.S. al Coda

Oh can't you__

✠ ***Coda***

F#m(add9)   **D**sus2   **E**sus2   **F#m**(add9)

Ev-'ry move__you make ev-'ry step__ you take, I'll be watch-ing you.

A(add9)   **F#m**(add9)   **D**sus2

Repeat ad. lib to fade

I'll be watch-ing you._____   I'll be watch-ing

46

The Final Countdown

Words & Music by Joey Tempest

> If you are playing this with another guitarist, one of you could try working out the original keyboard melody. The first few bars are shown in the TAB below.

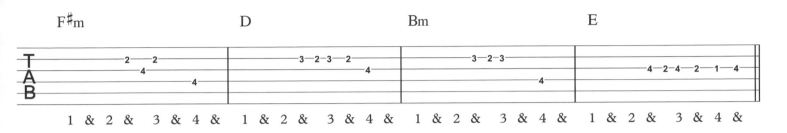

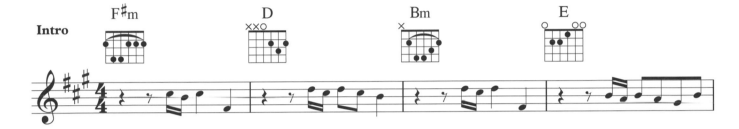

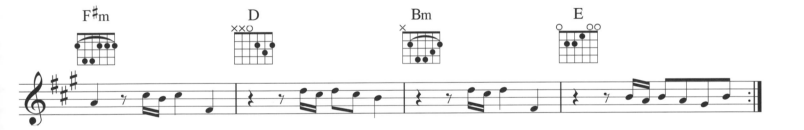

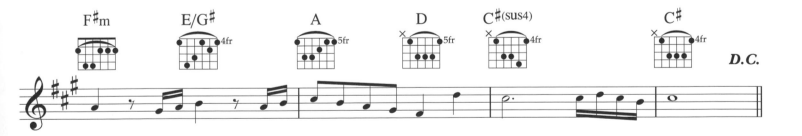

Verse

1. We're leav-ing__ to-ge-ther,   but still it's__ fare - well.__
2. We're head-ing__ for Ve - nus   and still we__ stand__ tall.__

And may-be__ we'll come back_____   to Earth.__ Who can tell?__
'Cause may-be__they've seen us_____   and wel - come us all.__

I guess there is   no one__ to blame.   We're leav-ing   ground.__ (leav-ing
With so ma-ny light years to   go   and things to be   found__ (to be

ground)__ Will things e - ver be_____ the same a - gain?   It's the fi-nal
found)__ I'm sure that__we'll all_____ miss her so.

Chorus

count-down,_____   the fi - nal

1.

count-down.__

48

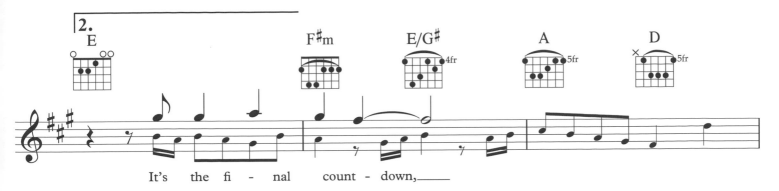

It's the fi - nal count - down,____

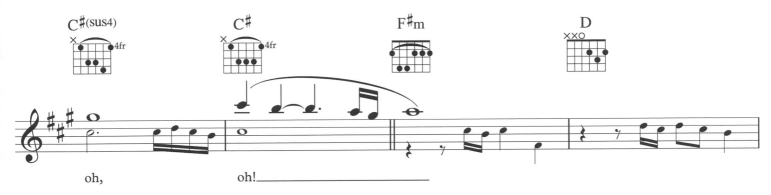

oh,   oh!____

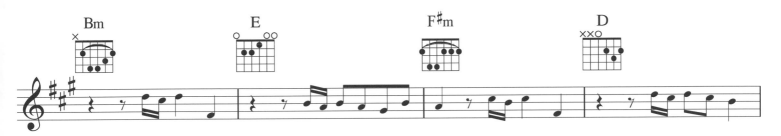

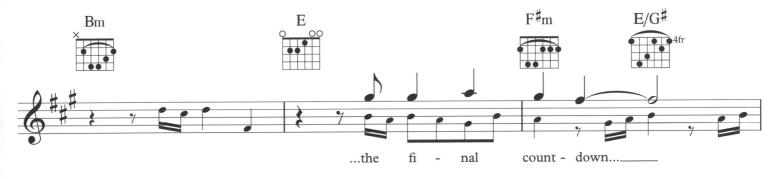

...the fi - nal count - down...____

Oh,____   It's the fi - nal

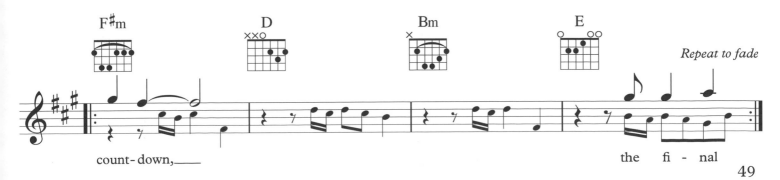

Repeat to fade

count-down,____   the fi - nal

49

Here I Go Again

Words & Music by David Coverdale & Bernie Marsden

Chorus strumming style:

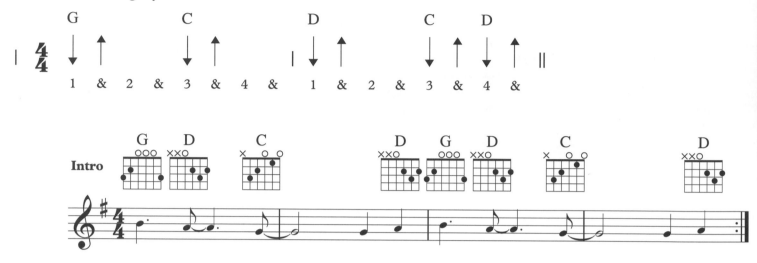

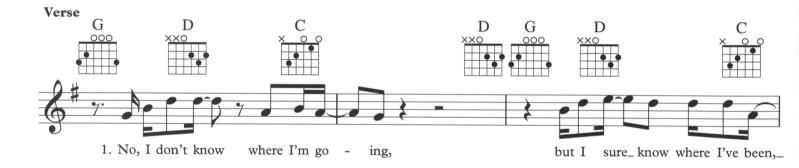

1. No, I don't know   where I'm go - ing,   but I   sure know where I've been,

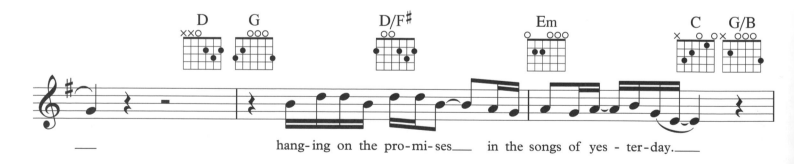

hang-ing on the pro-mi-ses___   in the songs of yes - ter-day.___

And I've made up my mind:___   I ain't was - ting no more time.___

2. Though I keep sear-ching for an ans - wer,
3. I'm just a-nother heart in need of re - scue,

I ne - ver seem to find what I'm look - ing for.
wait-ing on love's sweet cha - ri - ty._____

Oh Lord,_ I pray._ You give_ me strength_ to car - ry on_____
And I'm_ gon - na_ hold on_ for the_____ rest of_ my days,_____

'cause I know what it means_____ to walk a - long_ the lone-ly street_ of

Chorus

dreams. And here I go_ a - gain_ on my own,_____ go-ing

down the on - ly road_ I've e-ver known.___ Like a drif-ter I was born_ to walk a-lone._

And I've made up my mind.____

I ain't was - ting no more time.____ And

Outro

here I go____ a - gain____ on my own,_____ go - ing

down the on - ly road____ I've e - ver known._____ Like a

drif - ter I was born____ to walk a-lone.____ 'cause I know what it means____

Repeat to fade

_____ to walk a - long____ the lone - ly street____ of dreams. And

Heroes

Words by David Bowie
Music by David Bowie & Brian Eno

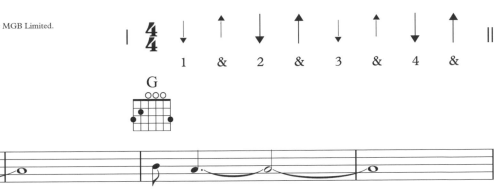

In the strumming rhythm below, the larger arrows show accented strums while the smaller ones are played softly.

Strumming style:

Intro

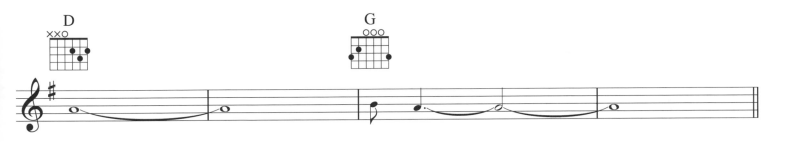

Verse

1. I,
2. I,

I wish you could swim,___
I will be king.___

like the dol - phins,
And__ you,__

like dol - phins can swim._
you will be queen._

Though no - thing,
Though no - thing

55

Hey Joe

Words & Music by Billy Roberts

1. Hey,___ Joe,___ uh where you go-in' with that gun in your hand?
(Verse 2 see block lyrics)

Hey,___ Joe, I said where you goin' with that gun

in your hand? Al-right. I'm go-in' down to shoot my old la-dy,

you know I caught her mess-in' 'round with an-oth-er man. Yeah.

I'm go-in' down to shoot my old la-dy, you know I caught her mess-in' 'round with an-

Guitar Solo

Verse

Verse 2:
Uh, hey Joe, I heard you shot your woman down,
You shot her down now.
Uh, hey Joe, I heard you shot your old lady down,
You shot her down in the ground, yeah.
Yes, I did, I shot her,
You know I caught her messin' 'round, messin' 'round town.
Yes, I did, I shot her,
You know I caught my old lady messin' 'round town,
And I gave her the gun, I shot her!

Highway To Hell

Words & Music by Angus Young, Malcolm Young & Bon Scott

To match recording tune guitar one semitone down

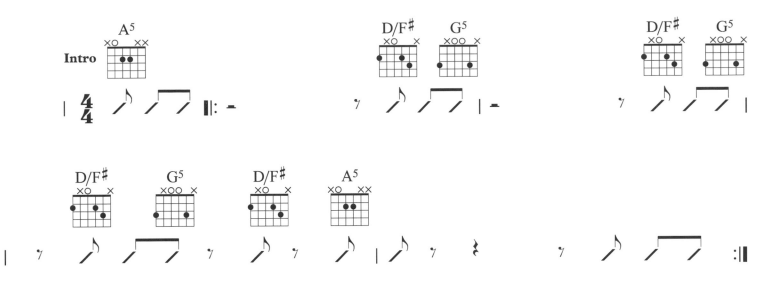

Don't stop me!___

Guitar Solo

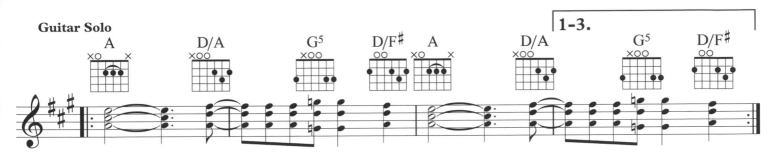

1-3.

4. **Chorus**

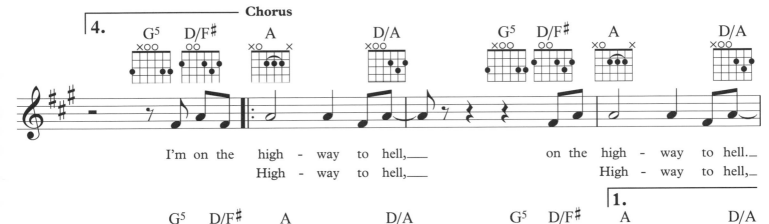

I'm on the high - way to hell,___ on the high - way to hell.___
High - way to hell,___ High - way to hell,___

1.

___ I'm on the high - way to hell,___ On the high - way to...
___ High - way to hell,___

2. **Outro**

High - way to... And I'm go - in' down___

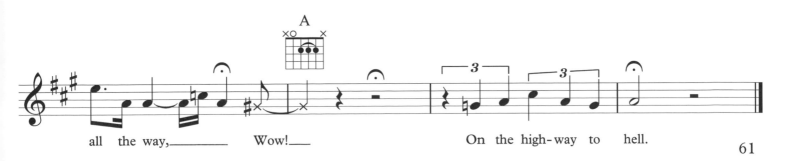

all the way,___ Wow!___ On the high - way to hell.

I Don't Want To Miss A Thing

Words & Music by Diane Warren

spent with you____ is a mo-ment I trea - sure.
stay with you____ in this mo-ment for-ev - er, for-ev - er and ev - er.____

Chorus

Don't wan-na close_ my eyes, don't wan-na fall____ a-sleep, 'cause I'd

miss you, ba-by, and I don't wan-na miss a thing.____ 'Cause ev-en when I dream of you,

To Coda ⊕

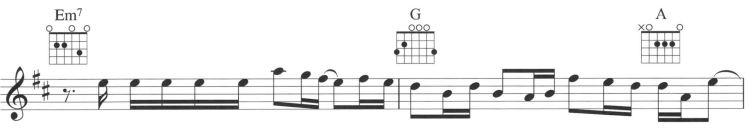

the sweet-est dream would nev - er do._ I'd still miss you, ba-by, and I don't wan-na miss a thing._

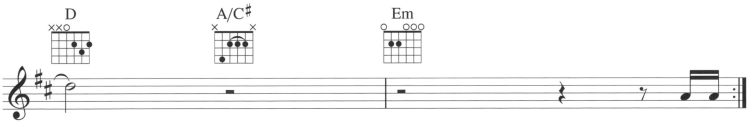

____

2. Lay-ing

⊕ *Coda*

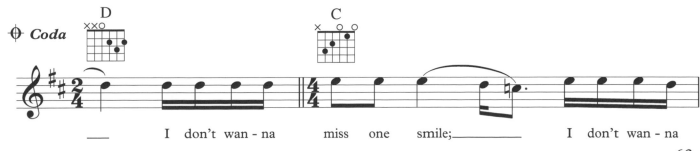

____ I don't wan - na miss one smile;____ ____ I don't wan - na

miss one kiss. I just wan-na be with you,___ right here___ with you,___

just like this. I just wan-na hold___ you close,_____ feel your heart so

close to mine,_____ and just stay here in___ this mo-ment for all the

rest of time.___ Ba - by, ba - by._____

Chorus

Don't wan-na close_ my eyes,_ don't wan-na fall___ a - sleep,_'cause I'd

miss you, ba - by, and I don't wan-na miss a thing.___ 'Cause ev - en when I dream of you,___

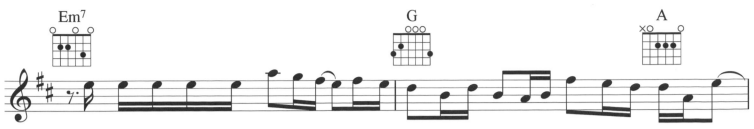

the sweet-est dream would nev-er do.— I'd still miss you, ba-by, and I don't wan-na miss a thing.—

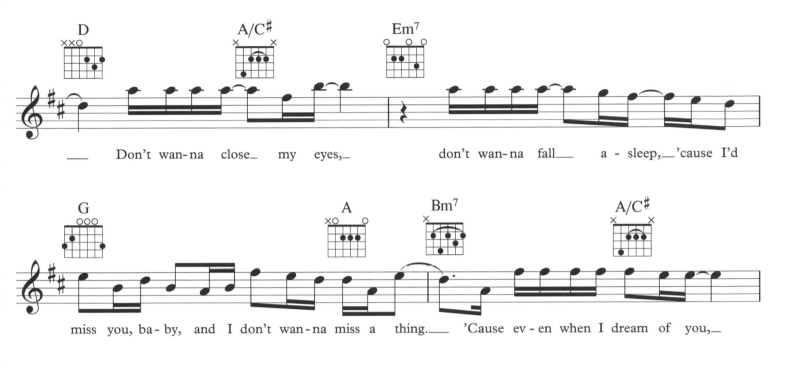

— Don't wan-na close— my eyes,— don't wan-na fall— a-sleep,—'cause I'd

miss you, ba-by, and I don't wan-na miss a thing.— 'Cause ev-en when I dream of you,—

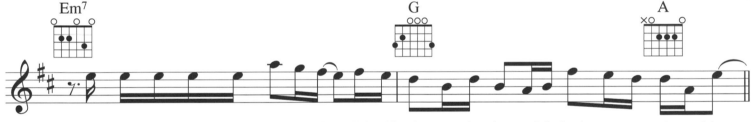

the sweet-est dream would nev-er do.— I'd still miss you, ba-by, and I don't wan-na miss a thing.—

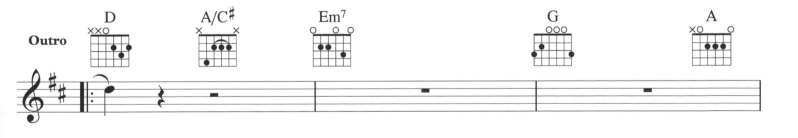

Outro

Repeat ad lib. to fade

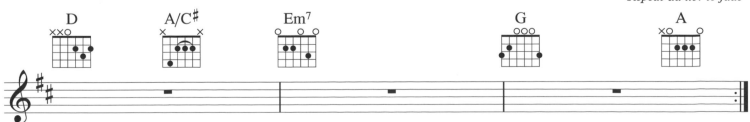

I Saw Her Standing There

Words & Music by John Lennon & Paul McCartney

Intro riff:

saw her stand - ing there.____   1.   2. Well, she____   2, 3.   Well, my

heart went boom____ when I crossed that room,____ and I

held her hand in mi - ne._____

_____ { Well, Oh, } we danced____ through the night____ and we

held each oth - er tight,____ And be - fore too long____ I____

__ fell in love with her.____ Now I'll nev - er dance_

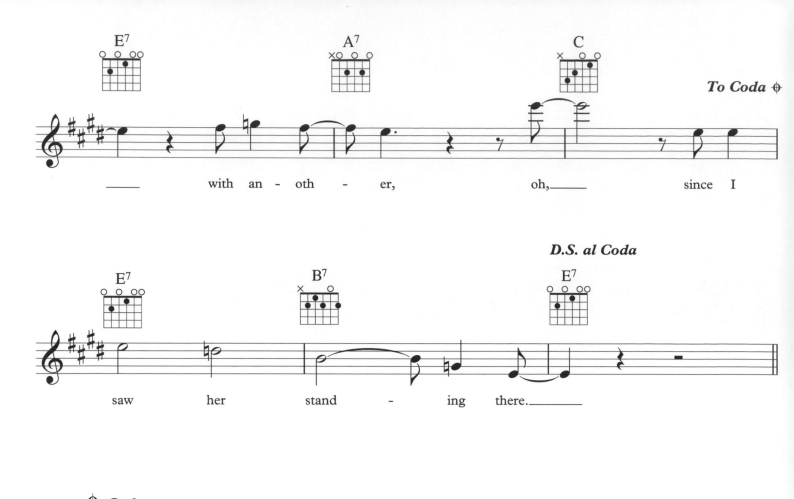

with an - oth - er, oh,_____ since I

D.S. al Coda

saw her stand - ing there._____

Coda

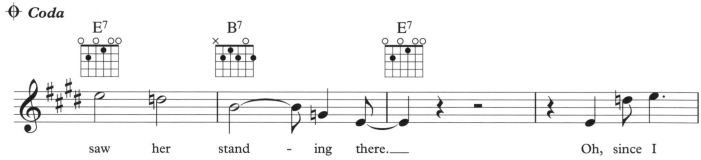

saw her stand - ing there.___ Oh, since I

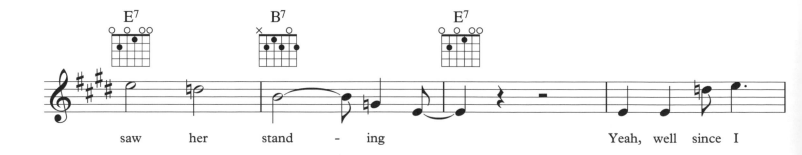

saw her stand - ing Yeah, well since I

68   saw her stand - ing there._____

I Want You To Want Me

Words & Music by Rick Nielsen

Verse strumming style:

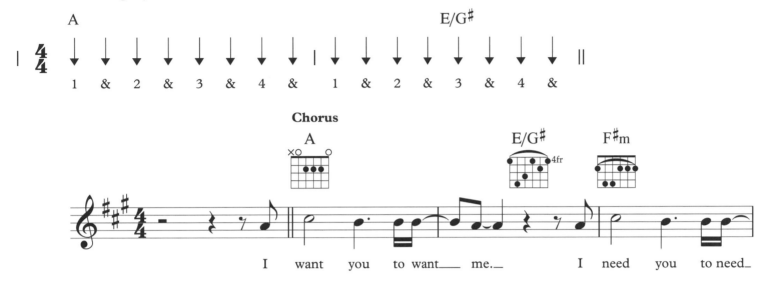

Chorus

If It Makes You Happy

Words & Music by Sheryl Crow & Jeffrey Trott

Intro

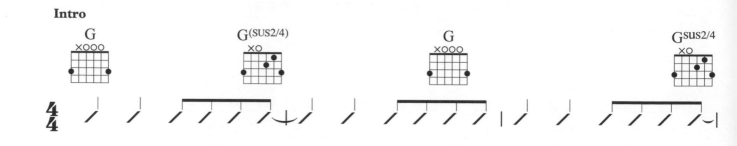

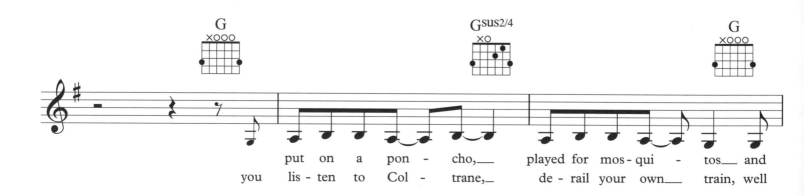

D Am C

If it makes you hap - py,___ then why the hell__ are you__ so

1.
G Gsus2/4 G Gsus2/4 G

sad?___ 2.You get down,

2, 3.
G Gsus2/4 G Am

To Coda ◈

sad?___ If it makes you hap - py.___

C G D Am

It can't be that bad.___ If it makes you hap - py,___

C Em

then why the hell__ are you__ so sad?___

Interlude

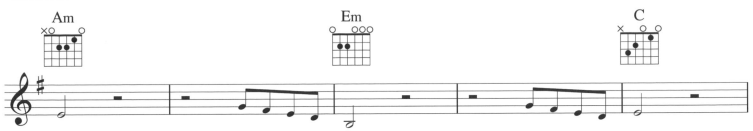

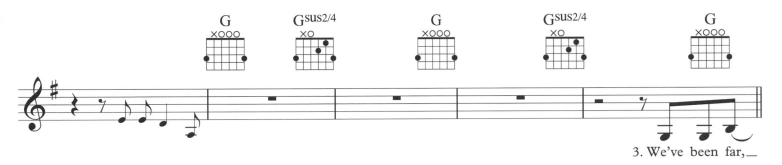

D.S. al Coda

D.S. al Coda

3. We've been far,__

Coda

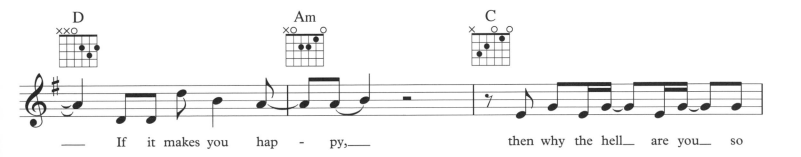

- py.__ It can't be that bad.__

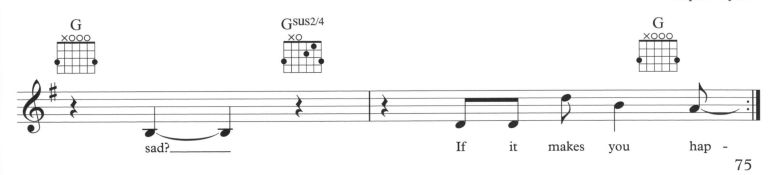

__ If it makes you hap - py,__ then why the hell__ are you__ so

Repeat to fade

sad?__ If it makes you hap -

75

Jessie's Girl

Words & Music by Rick Springfield

Bridge

And I'm look-in' in the mir - ror all the time_____ won-drin' what she don't see_

_ in_____ me. I've been fun-ny, I've been cool_____ with the lines._____

Interlude

Ain't that the way love's sup-posed_____ to_____ be?

1.

2.

Tell me where can I find a_____ wom-an like_____ that?

Guitar Solo

Lithium

Words & Music by Kurt Cobain

Chorus

mor- ning is eve-ry-day___ for all___ I care.___ And I'm not scared.___ Light my
-ci - ted, I can't wait___ to meet you there.___ But I don't care.___ I'm so

can - dles, in a daze___ 'cause I've found god.___ Yeah,___
hor - ny, but that's o- kay.___ My will___ is good.___

yeah.___ Yeah,___

yeah.___ Yeah,___

yeah.___

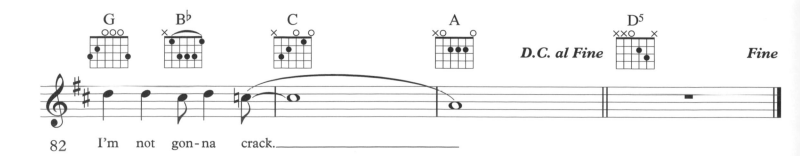

82 I'm not gon-na crack.

Livin' On A Prayer

Words & Music by Jon Bon Jovi, Richie Sambora & Desmond Child

(Guitar riff)

(*Spoken:*) Once upon a time, not so long ago...

Verse

1. Tom‑my used to work on the docks,_____ un‑ion's been on strike. He's_____
2. Tom‑my's got his six‑ string in hock,_____ now he's_____ hold‑ing in when he

down on his luck, it's tough,_____ so tough.
used to make it talk. So tough,_____ it's tough.

_____ Gi‑na works the din‑er all day_____
_____ Gi‑na dreams of run‑ning a‑way;_____ when

Instrumental

Liv- in' on____ a prayer._____

Oh,_____ we've got to

hold__ on__ read-y or__ not,   you live for the fight when it's   all that you've got.

Chorus

Wo,_____ we're half- way there.____ Wo,_____   liv - in' on a prayer.__

Repeat to fade

Take my   hand__ and we'll make it, I   swear.__ Wo,_____   liv - in' on a prayer.__

London Calling

Words & Music by Joe Strummer, Mick Jones, Paul Simonon & Topper Headon

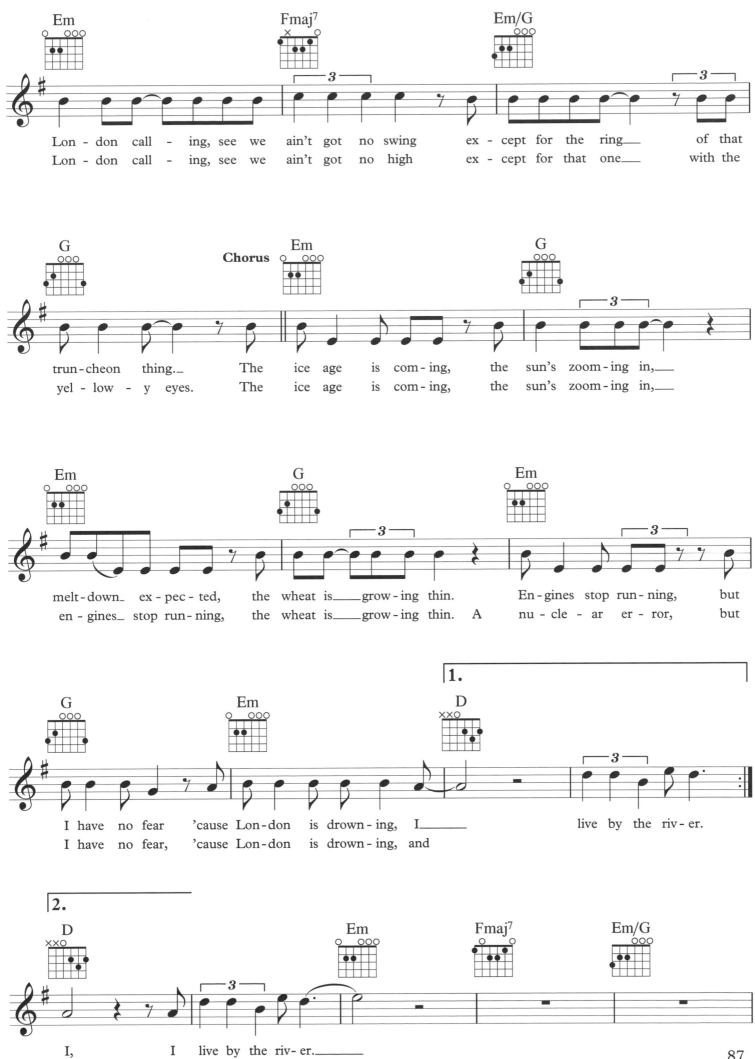

Money For Nothing

Words & Music by Mark Knopfler & Sting

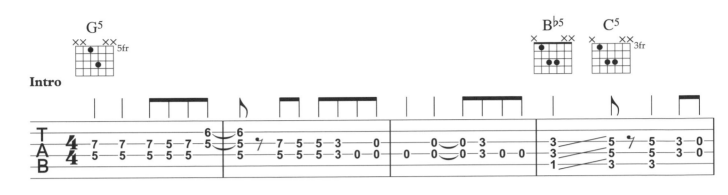

Intro

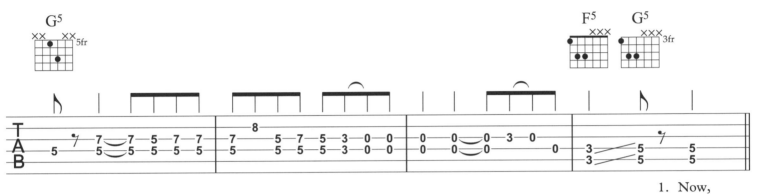

1. Now,

Verse

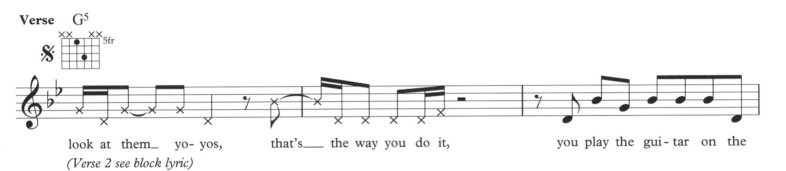

look at them_ yo- yos,   that's_ the way you do it,   you play the gui- tar on the

(Verse 2 see block lyric)

M.   T.   V._   That ain't_____ work- in',   that's_ the way you do it,

mon- ey   for no- thin' and your chicks   for free._   Now that ain't work- in',   that's_

the way you do it, let me tell ya them guys ain't dumb. You

may-be get a blis-ter on your lit-tle fin-ger, may-be get a blis-ter on your thumb.

Chorus

We got-ta in-stall mic-ro-wave ov-ens, cus-tom kit-chen de-

-li-ve-ries. We got-ta move these re-fri-ge-ra-tors,

we got-ta move these co-lour T. V.s Ow!

Interlude
(as Intro)

To Coda

90

that ain't work- in'   that's the way you do it,   you play the gui-tar on the M. T. V.

That ain't work- in',   that's___ the way you do it,   mon-ey for no- thin' and your chicks   for free.

Mo- ney   for no- thin'   and your chicks for   free.___   Get your

mon- ey   for no -thin'   and your chicks for   free.___

Verse 2:
I should have learned to play the guitar,
I should have learned to play them drums,
Look at that mama, she got it stickin' in the camera.
Man, we could have some fun.
And he's up there, what's that? Hawaiian noises?
He's bangin' on the bongos like a chimpanzee,
Oh that ain't workin', that's the way you do it,
Get your money for nothin', get your chicks for free.

More Than A Feeling

Words & Music by Tom Scholz

Verse

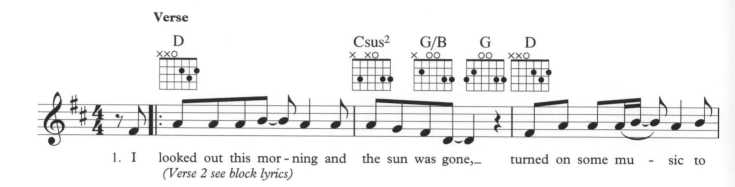

1. I looked out this mor - ning and the sun was gone,__ turned on some mu - sic to
(Verse 2 see block lyrics)

start my____ day.__ I lost my - self____ in a fa - mil - iar song, I

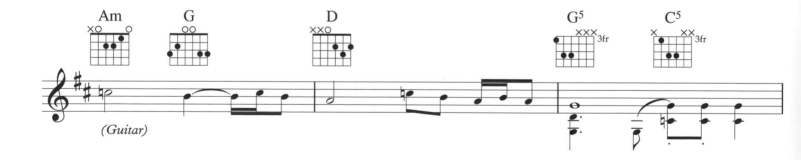

closed my____ eyes____ and I slipped a - way._____

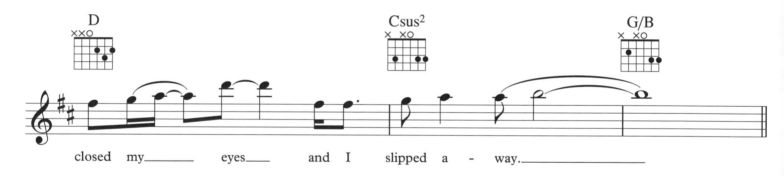

(Guitar)

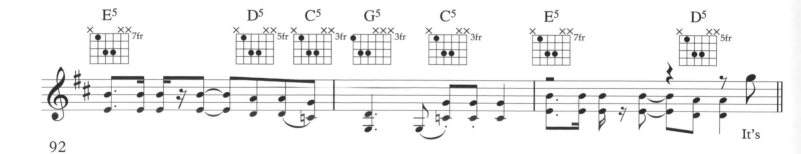

It's

Chorus

more than a feel - ing, when I hear that old song ___ they used to play. ___

To Coda ⊕

I be - gin dream - ing, when I see Mar - i - anne ___ walk a - way.

1.

I see my Mar - i - anne walk-ing a - way. ___

(Bass)

2.

Guitar Solo

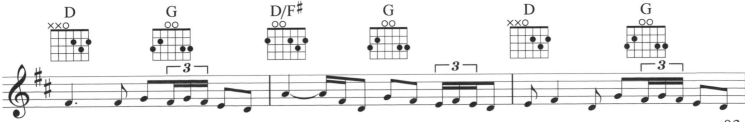

93

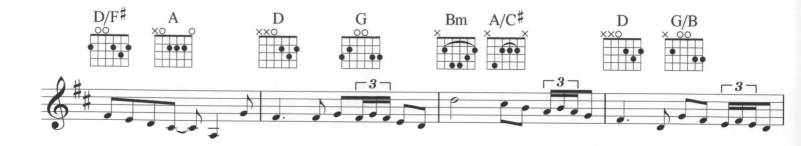

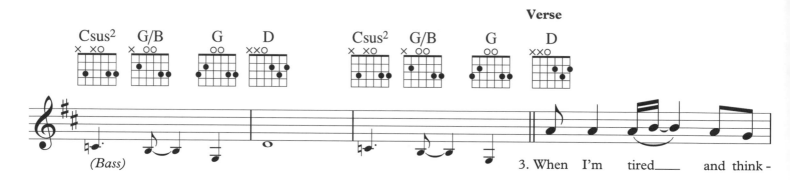

Verse

(Bass)   3. When I'm tired___ and think-

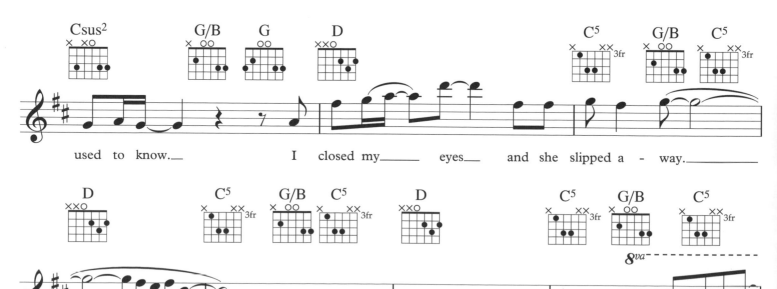

-ing cold   I hide in my mu - sic, for-get the__ day,_ and dream of a girl___   I

used to know.___   I closed my_____ eyes___ and she slipped a - way.___

She slipped a - way__

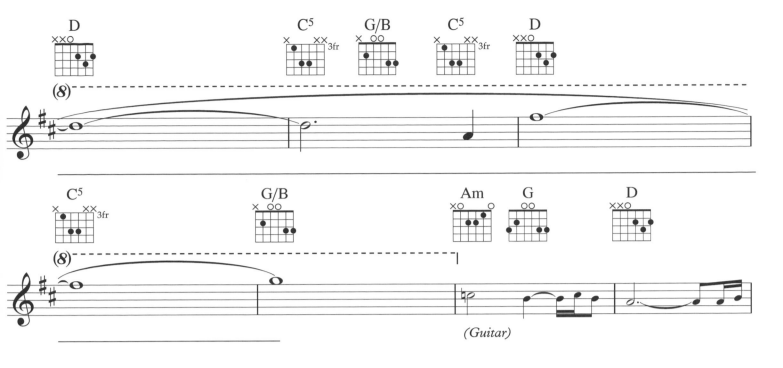

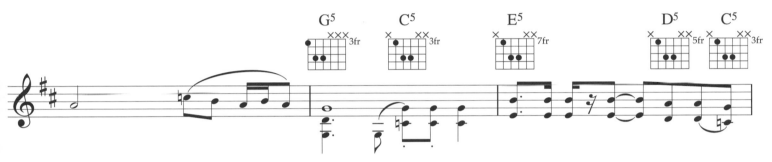

(Guitar)

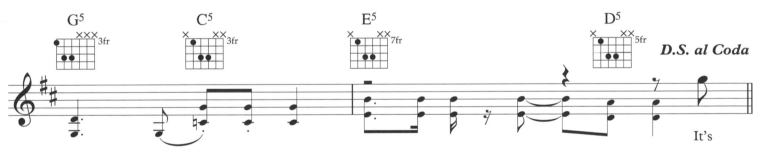

D.S. al Coda

It's

⊕ **Coda**

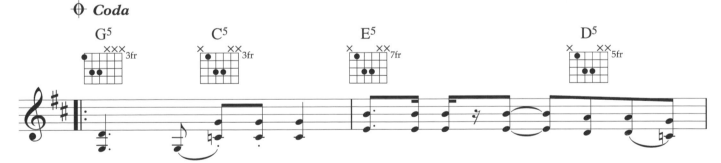

Repeat to fade

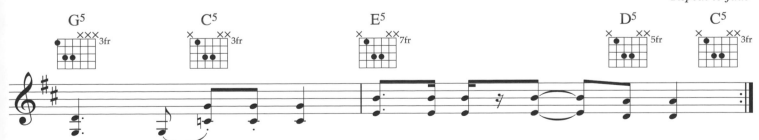

Verse 2:
So many people have come and gone,
Their faces fade as the years go by,
Yet I still recall as I wander on,
As clear as the sun in the summer sky.

Paperback Writer

Words & Music by John Lennon & Paul McCartney

Intro riff:

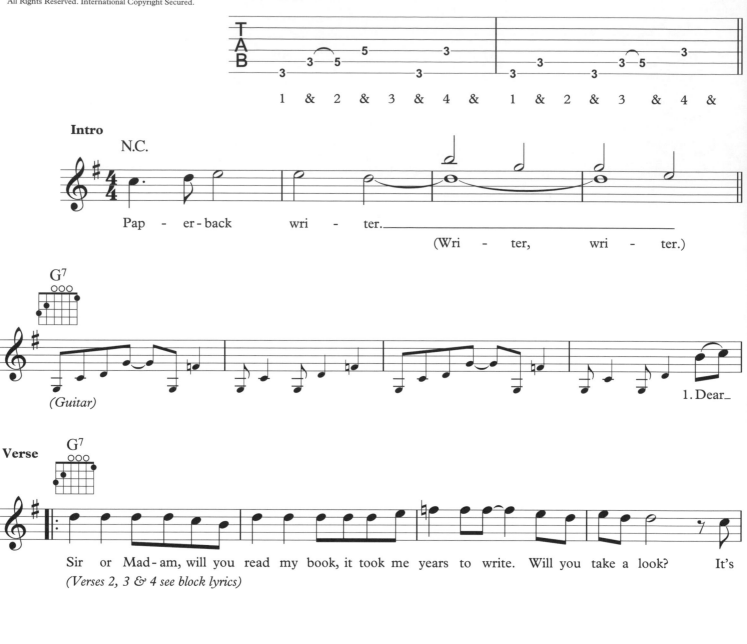

Intro

N.C.

Pap - er - back wri - ter._____ (Wri - ter, wri - ter.)

G⁷

(Guitar)

1. Dear__

Verse G⁷

Sir or Mad - am, will you read my book, it took me years to write. Will you take a look? It's
(Verses 2, 3 & 4 see block lyrics)

based on a nov-el by a man named Lear and I need a job,__ so I want to be a pa-per-back

1. **2.**

C G⁷ G⁷

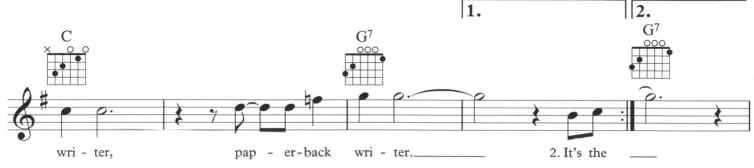

wri - ter, pap - er - back wri - ter._____ 2. It's the __

N.C.

Pap - er-back wri - ter._____ (Guitar)
(Pap - er-back wri - ter, wri - ter.)

3.

3. It's a ___ If you

4.

___ Pap - er-back wri - ter._____
(Pap - er-back wri - ter, wri - ter.) (Guitar)

G⁷

Repeat to fade

Pap - er - back wri - ter._____
(Pap - er - back wri - ter.)_____

Verse 2:
It's the dirty story of a dirty man,
And his clinging wife doesn't understand.
His son is working for the Daily Mail,
It's a steady job,
But he wants to be a paperback writer,
Paperback writer.

Verse 3:
It's a thousand pages give or take a few,
I'll be writing more in a week or two.
I can make it longer if you like the style,
I can change it 'round,
And I want to be a paperback writer,
Paperback writer.

Verse 4:
If you really like it you can have the rights,
It could make a million for you overnight.
If you must return it you can send it here,
But I need a break,
And I want to be a paperback writer,
Paperback writer.

97

Mr. Brightside

Written by Brandon Flowers & Dave Keuning

Capo: Fret 1

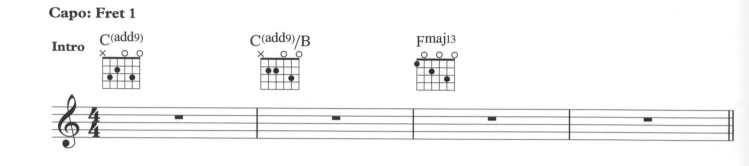

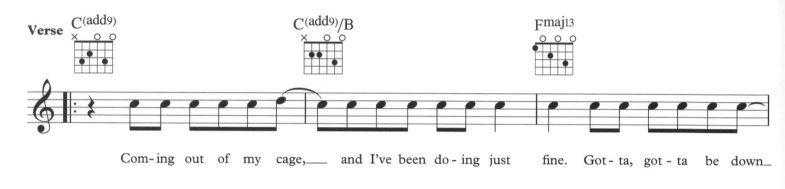

Com-ing out of my cage,___ and I've been do-ing just fine. Got-ta, got-ta be down___

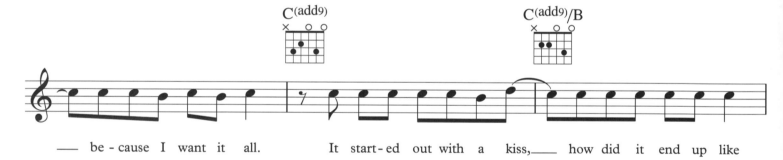

___ be-cause I want it all. It start-ed out with a kiss,___ how did it end up like

this? It was on-ly a kiss,___ it was on-ly a kiss. Now I'm fall-ing a-sleep___

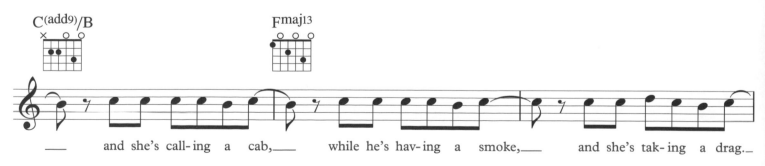

___ and she's call-ing a cab,___ while he's hav-ing a smoke,___ and she's tak-ing a drag.

Now they're go-ing to bed___ and my sto-mach is sick,___ and it's all in his head___

Bridge

___ but she's touch-ing his chest now. He takes off her dress now,

let - ting me go.___

And I just can't look; it's kill - ing me and

tak - ing___ con - trol.

Chorus

Jea - lou - sy turn - ing saints in to the sea, turn - ing through sick

lul - la - bies,   chok - ing___ on___ your___ a - li - bies.   But   it's   just   the

price   I   pay,___   des - ti - ny   is   call - ing   me.   Op - en   up   my

ea - ger___   eyes,_____   'cause   I'm   Mis - ter   Bright - side.

1.   **2.**

I   nev - er.___

1-3.   **4.**

I

The Passenger

Words by James Osterberg
Music by James Osterberg & Ricky Gardiner

Strumming style:

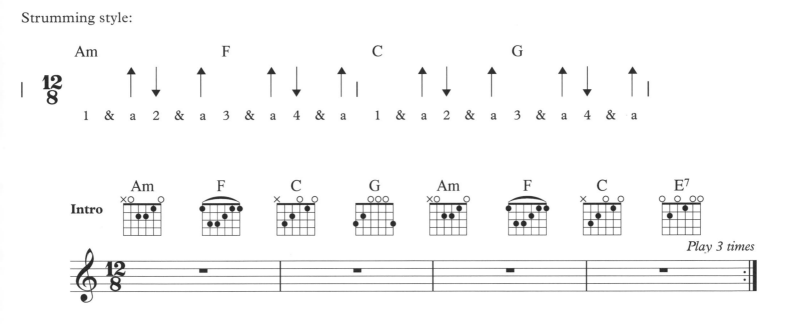

Verse

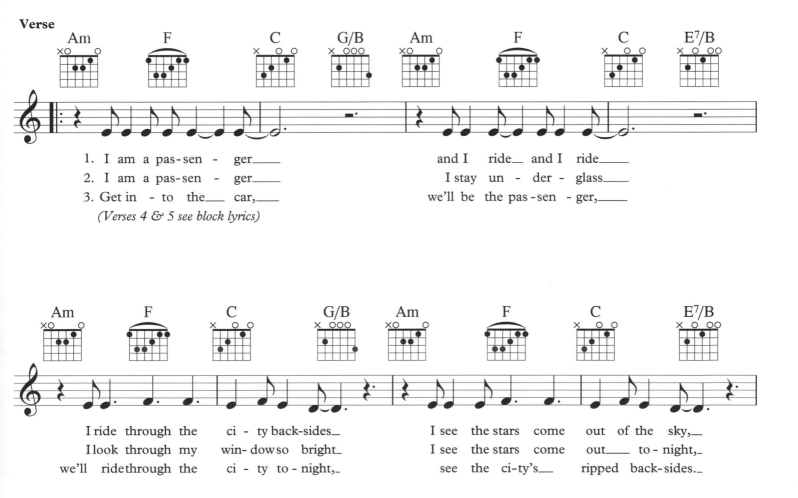

1. I am a pas-sen - ger___ and I ride__ and I ride___
2. I am a pas-sen - ger___ I stay un - der - glass___
3. Get in - to the__ car,___ we'll be the pas-sen - ger,___

(Verses 4 & 5 see block lyrics)

I ride through the ci-ty back-sides__ I see the stars come out of the sky,__
I look through my win-dow so bright__ I see the stars come out__ to-night,__
we'll ride through the ci-ty to-night,__ see the ci-ty's__ ripped back-sides.__

Verse 4: play 5 times
Verse 5: play 4 times

I hear the bright and hol-low__ sky,__ you know it looks so good to-night.__
I see the bright and hol-low__ sky,__ ov-er the ci - ty's ripped back sky.__
We'll see the bright and hol-low__ sky,__ we'll see the stars that shine so bright,

1.

2, 4-5.

And ev - 'ry-thing looks good to - night.__ I sing,

Chorus

la, la, la, la, la, la, la, la,__ la, la, la, la,

la, la, la, la,__ la, la, la, la, la, la, la, la,__ la, la, la.

Verse 4
Oh, the passenger,
How, how he rides.
Oh, the passenger,
He rides and he rides.
He looks through his window,
What does he see?
He sees the sight of hollow sky,
He sees the stars come out tonight,
He sees the city's ripped backsides,
He sees the winding ocean drive.
And everything was made for you and me,
All of it was made for you and me,
But it just belongs to you and me.
So let's take a ride and see what's mine.

I say, la, la, la, la, la, la, la, la,
La, la, la, la, la, la, la, la,
La, la, la, la, la, la, la, la, la, la, la.

Verse 5
Oh, the passenger,
He rides and he rides,
He sees things from under glass,
He looks through his window side,
He sees the things he knows are his,
He sees the bright and hollow sky,
He sees the city sleep at night,
He sees the skies are out tonight.
And all of it is yours and mine,
And all of it is yours and mine,
So let's ride and ride and ride and ride.

I say, la, la, la, la, la, la, la, la,
La, la, la, la, la, la, la, la,
La, la, la, la, la, la, la, la, la, la, la, la, etc.

Rock And Roll All Nite

Words & Music by Paul Stanley & Gene Simmons

> The chords shown in this song have a 'pushed' or anticipated feel—meaning that they're generally played a half-beat before the beginning of the bar.

To match recording tune guitar one semitone down

Intro

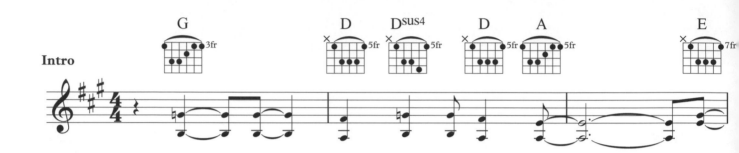

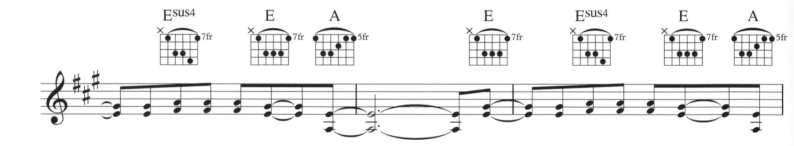

Verse

1. You show us eve-ry-thing you've got.___ You keep on dan-cin' and the
3. You keep on sa-ying you'll be mine for a while. You're loo-kin' fan-cy and I

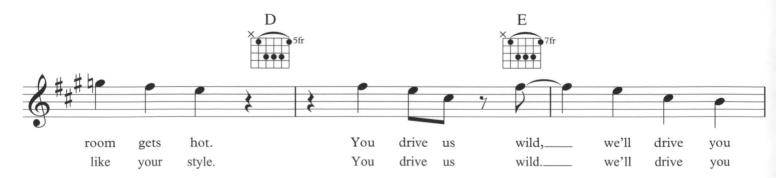

room gets hot. You drive us wild,___ we'll drive you
like your style. You drive us wild.___ we'll drive you

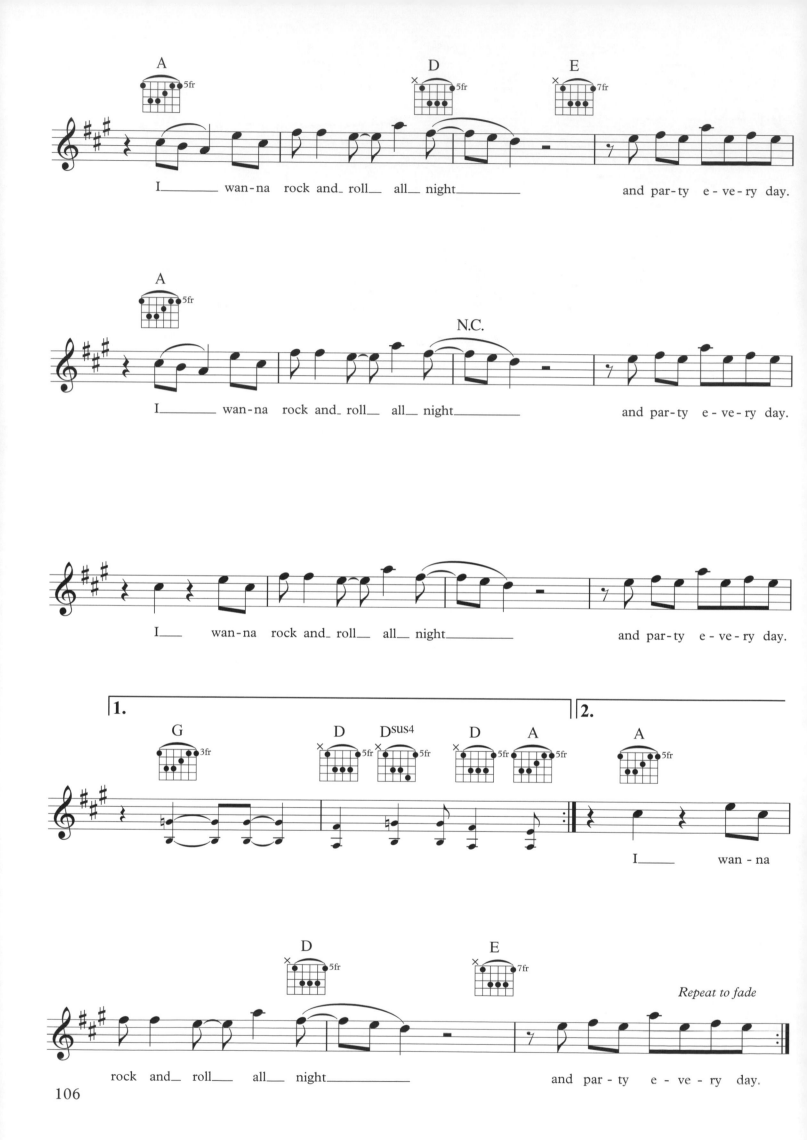

Roxanne

Words & Music by Sting

- anne,___ you don't have to wear that dress___ to - night,___
know my mind is made up so put a - way your make up,_____

walk the streets_ for___mo-ney,_ you don't care___ if it's wrong or if it's right. Rox -
told you once I won't_ tell you a-gain it's a crime___ the way...

Pre-Chorus

- anne,_____ you don't have to put on the red_____ light._____ Rox -

- anne,_____ you don't have to put on the red_____ light.

(Rox - anne.)_

Chorus

Put on the red_ light.
(Rox - anne.)_____

Put on the red_____ light.
(Rox - anne.)_____

108

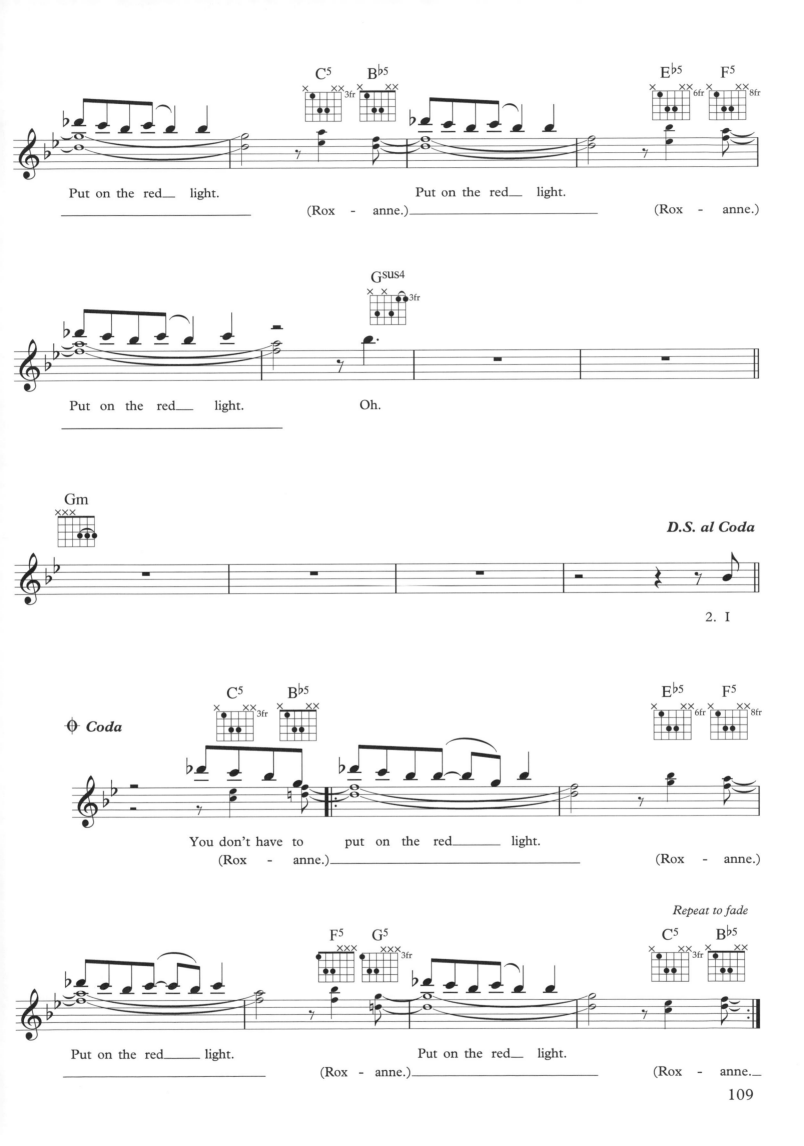

Sex On Fire

Words & Music by Caleb Followill, Nathan Followill, Jared Followill & Matthew Followill

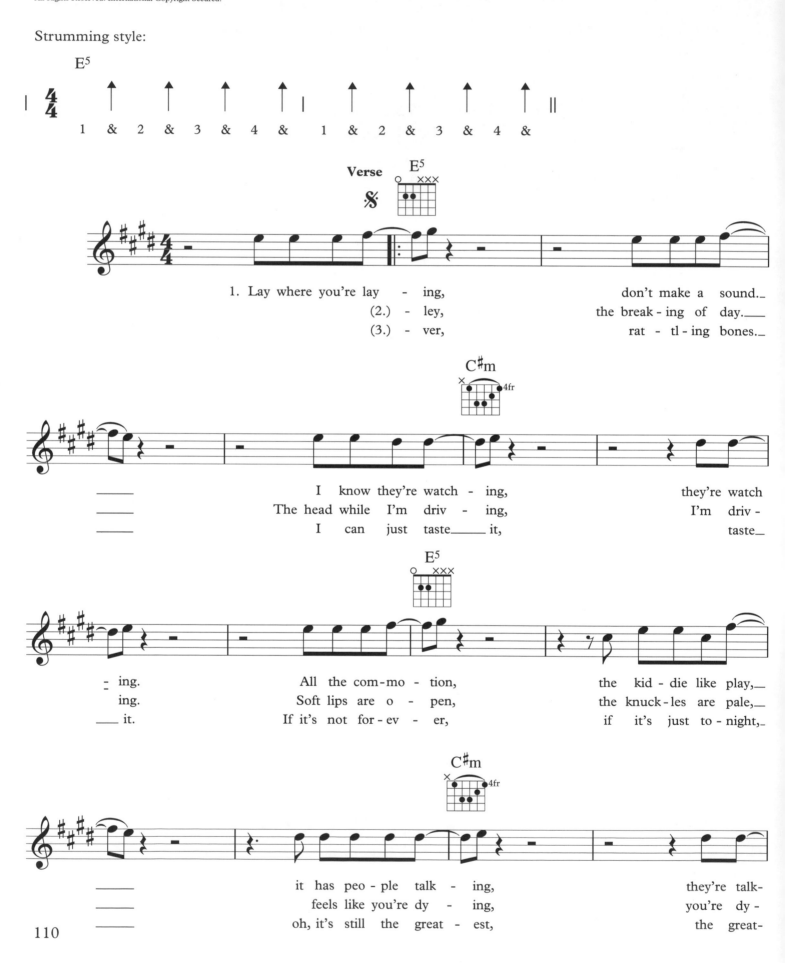

Should I Stay Or Should I Go

Words & Music by Mick Jones & Joe Strummer

So you've got to let me know:_   should I stay or should I
well, come on and let me know:_

1, 3.
go?   2. It's al - ways tease, tease,   should I stay or should I
       4. *Instrumental*   should I stay or should I

2, 4.

go now?   Should I stay or should I   go now?
(Chorus 2 see block lyrics)

If I go there will be trou - ble,_____   and if I stay it will be

To Coda

dou - ble.   So come on and let me   know:_____
          So you got - ta let me

D.S. al Coda

3. This in - de - ci - sion's bug - ging

114

⊕ _Coda_

know:_____ should I cool it or should I blow?

Should I stay or should I go now? If I go there will be trou ble,_____

and if I stay it will be dou-ble. So you got-ta let me

know:_____ Should I stay or should I go?

Verse 3
This indecision's bugging me
(Esta indecision me molesta)
If you don't want me, set me free
(Si no me quieres, librame)
Exactly who'm I supposed to be
(Digame que teno ser)
Don't you know which clothes even fit me?
(¿No sabes que ropas me queda?)
Come on and let me know
(Me tienes que desir)
Should I cool it or should I blow?
(¿Me debo ir o quedarme?)

Chorus 2
Should I stay or should I go now?
(¿Yo me frio o lo soplo?)
Should I stay or should I go now?
(¿Yo me frio o lo soplo?)
If I go there will be trouble
(Si me voy a ver peligro)
And if I stay it will be double
(Si me quedo sera el doble)
So you gotta let me know
(Me tienes que decir)...

Since You've Been Gone

Words & Music by Russ Ballard

This version is from Rainbow's 1979 album *Down To Earth*. However, to play along with their single version of this song, you'll need to put a capo on the 1st fret.

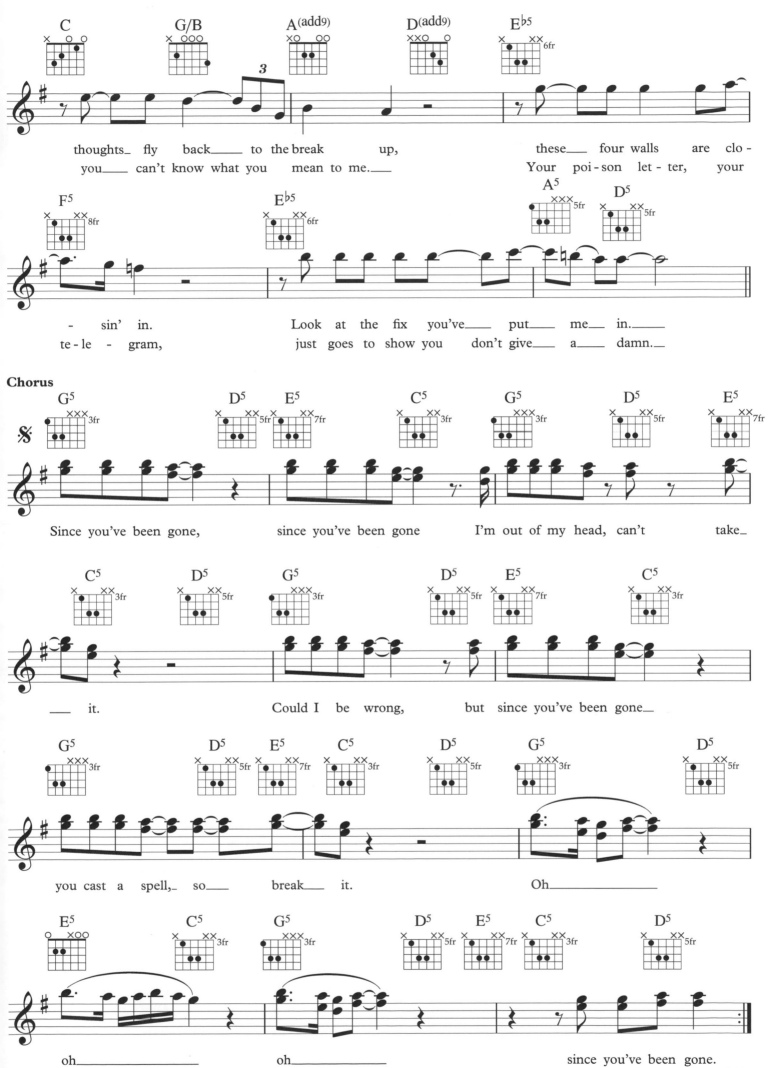

117

Bridge

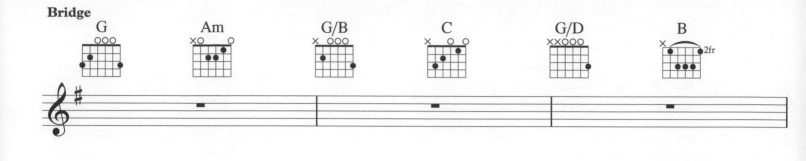

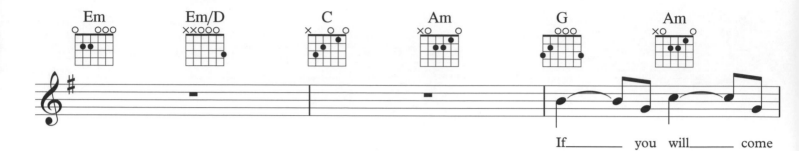

If_____ you will_____ come

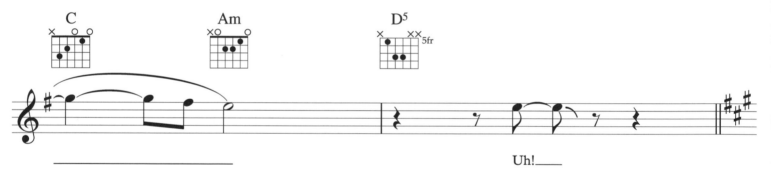

back,   ba - by you know   you'd nev - er be   wrong._____

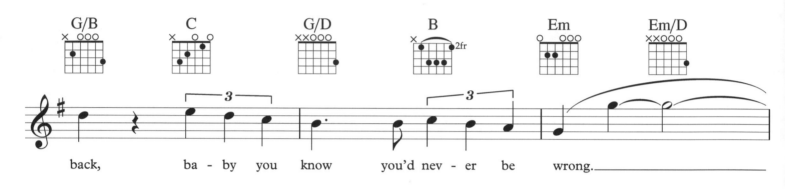

Uh!_____

Chorus

Since you've been gone,__   since you've been gone,   I'm out of my head, can't   take

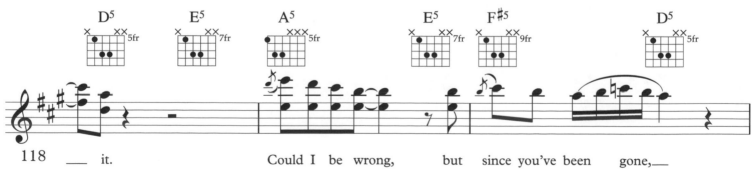

118 __ it.   Could I be wrong,   but since you've been   gone,__

you cast a spell_ so___ break_ it.___ Oh_____

oh_____ oh_____ oh_____

ev - er since you've been gone._____

Guitar Solo

Outro Chorus

Since you've been gone,___ since you've been gone,___ I'm

out of my head, can't take___ it.

119

Song 2

Music by Damon Albarn, Graham Coxon, Alex James & David Rowntree

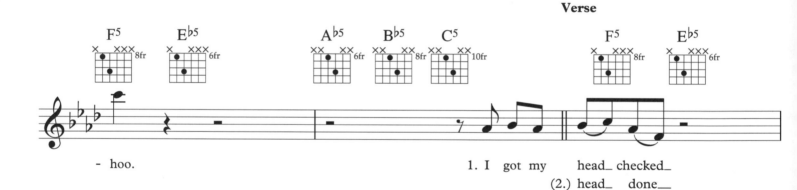

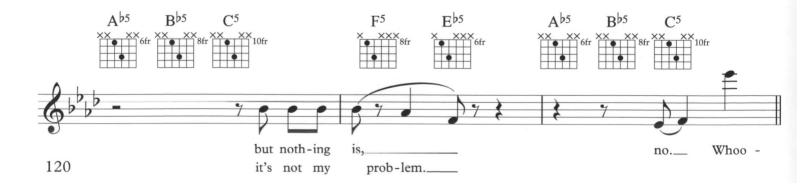

Smells Like Teen Spirit

Words & Music by Kurt Cobain, Dave Grohl & Krist Novoselic

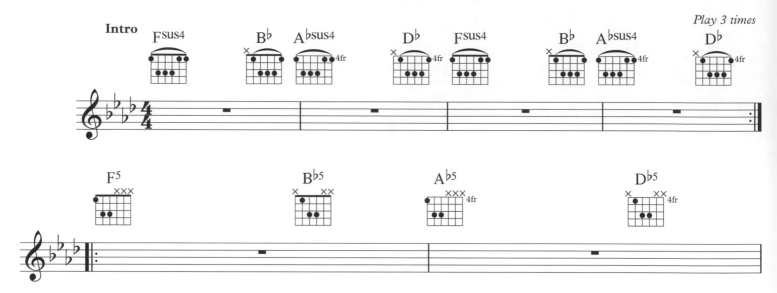

1. Load up___ on guns,___ bring___ your friends,___ it's fun___ to lose___
2. I'm worse_ at what___ I___ do best___ and for___ this gift___
3. And I___ for - get___ just why___ I taste,___ oh yeah,_ I guess___

___ and to___ pre - tend.___ She's ov - er - bored__ and self - as - sured,___
___ I_ feel___ blessed._ Our lit - tle group__ has al - ways been___
___ it makes___ me smile.___ I found it hard,___ it's hard___ to find,___

___ oh no,___ I know___ a dir - ty word.___
___ and al - ways will___ un - til___ the end.___
___ oh well,___ what - ev - er, nev - er mind.___

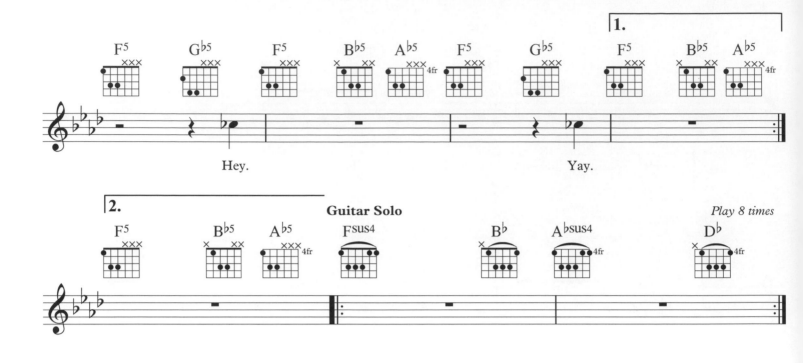

Hey.   Yay.

Guitar Solo   *Play 8 times*

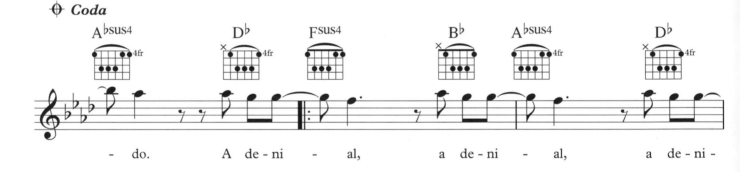

D.S. al Coda

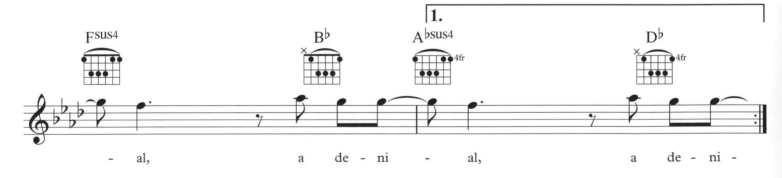

🟦 *Coda*

- do.   A de - ni - al,   a de - ni - al,   a de - ni -

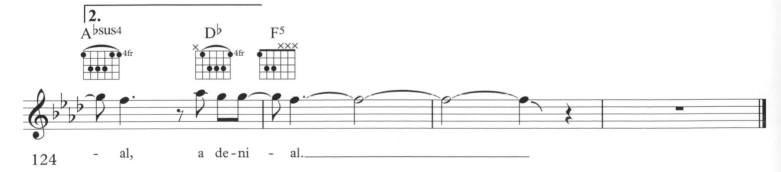

- al,   a de - ni - al,   a de - ni -

- al,   a de - ni - al.

Substitute

Words & Music by Pete Townshend

Intro riff:

Verse

1. You think we look pret-ty good to-geth - er.___
2. (D.C.) I was born with a plas - tic spoon in my mouth.

You think my shoes are made of leath - er.___ But I'm a
The north side in my town faced east and the east was fac - ing south.. And now you

sub - sti - tute___ for an - oth - er guy. I look pret-ty tall but my
dare to look___ me in___ the eye. Those croco - dile tears are what

heels are high. The sim - ple things you see are all com - pli - ca - ted. I
you cry. It's a gen - u - ine prob - lem. You won't try___ to

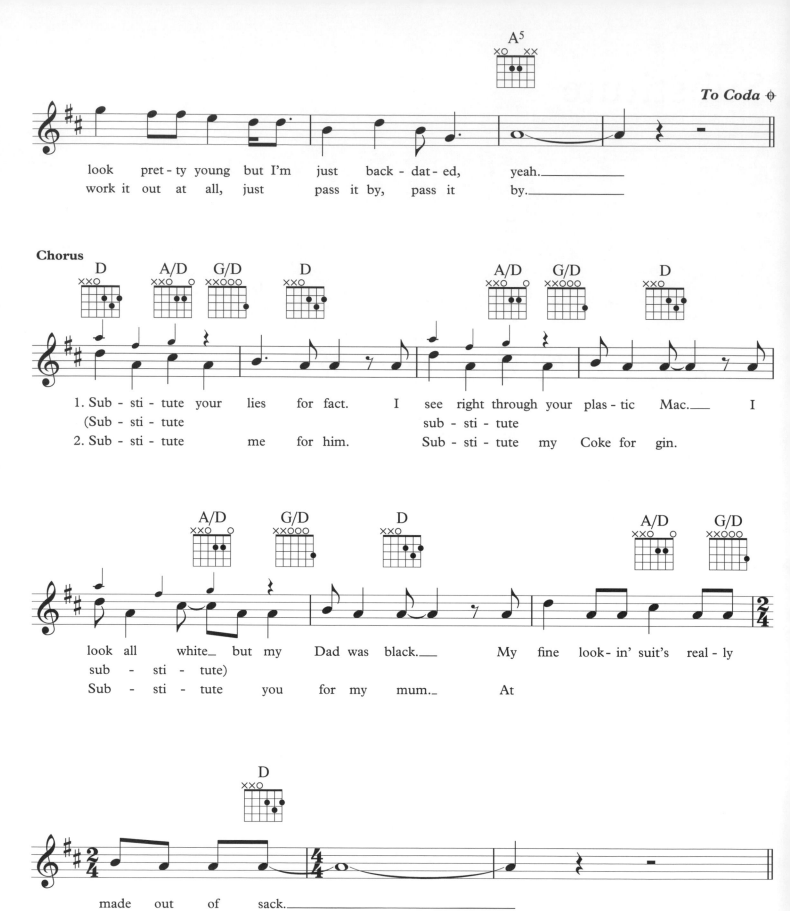

To Coda ⊕

look pret - ty young but I'm just back - dat - ed, yeah._____

work it out at all, just pass it by, pass it by._____

Chorus

D   A/D   G/D   D   A/D   G/D   D

1. Sub - sti - tute your lies for fact. I see right through your plas - tic Mac.___ I
   (Sub - sti - tute   sub - sti - tute
2. Sub - sti - tute me for him. Sub - sti - tute my Coke for gin.

A/D   G/D   D   A/D   G/D

look all white__ but my Dad was black.___ My fine look - in' suit's real - ly
sub - sti - tute)
Sub - sti - tute you for my mum.__ At

D

made out of sack._____

Instrumental

N.C.

1.

126

Chorus

I'm a sub-sti-tute_ for an-oth-er guy._ I look pret-ty tall but my

heels are high._ The sim-ple things you see are all com-pli-cat-ed. I

D.C. al Coda

look pret-ty young but I'm just back-dat-ed, yeah._____

Coda

Chorus

(Sub-sti-tute) me for him. (Sub-sti-tute) my Coke for gin.
(Sub-sti-tute) your lies for fact. I see right through your plas-tic Mac. I
(Sub-sti-tute)

(Sub-sti-tute) you for my mum. At least I'll get my
look all white but my dad was black. My fine look-in' suit is real-ly
(Sub-sti-tute)

1.

wash-ing done._

2.

made out of sack._

127

Sultans Of Swing

Words & Music by Mark Knopfler

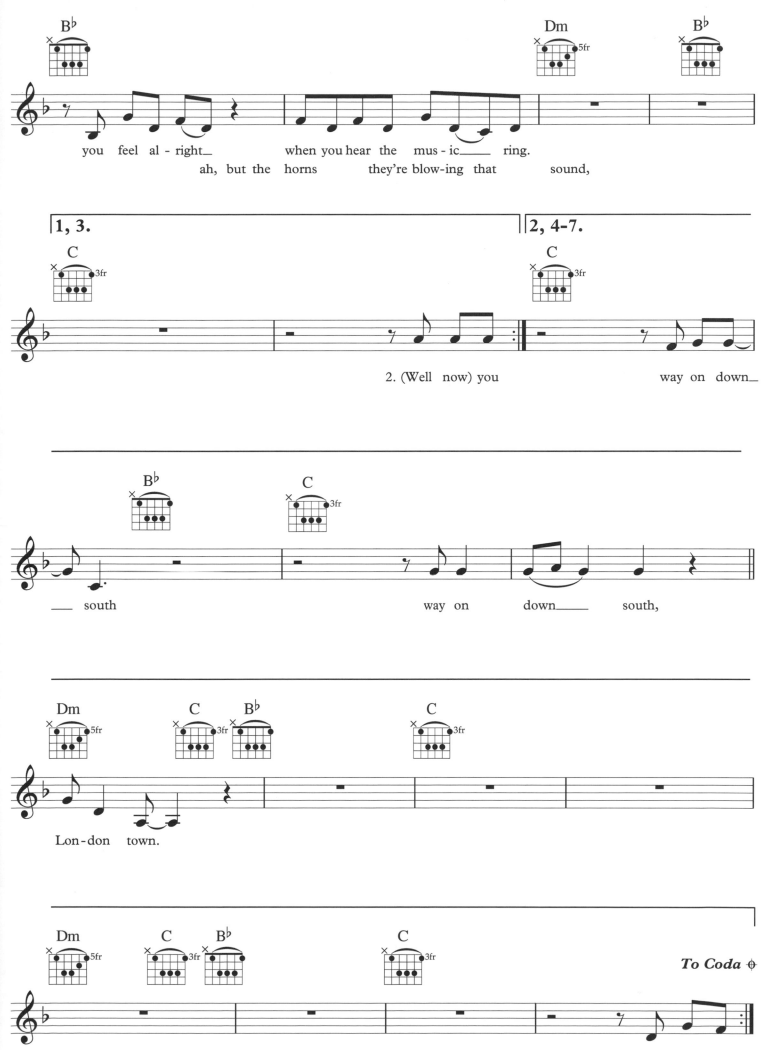

you feel al-right___ when you hear the mus-ic___ ring.
ah, but the horns they're blow-ing that sound,

1, 3.
2, 4-7.

2. (Well now) you
way on down___

___ south
way on down___ south,

Lon-don town.

To Coda

3. You check out

Coda

Guitar Solo

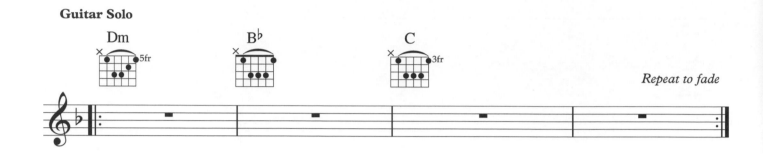

Repeat to fade

Verse 3
You check out Guitar George, he knows all the chords,
Mind he's strictly rhythm, he doesn't want to make it to cry or sing.
Yes, and an old guitar is all he can afford
When he gets up under the lights to play his thing.

Verse 4
And Harry doesn't mind if he doesn't make the scene,
He's got a daytime job, he's doing alright.
He can play the honky-tonk like anything,
Saving it up Friday night,
With the Sultans, with the Sultans of Swing.

Verse 5
And a crowd of young boys, they're fooling around in the corner,
Drunk and dressed in their best brown baggies and their platform soles.
They don't give a damn about any trumpet-playing band,
It ain't what they call rock and roll.
And the Sultans, yeah the Sultans they play Creole.

Verse 6 (Instrumental)

Verse 7
And then the man he steps right up to the microphone,
And says at last just as the time bell rings.
'Goodnight, now it's time to go home.'
And he makes it fast with one more thing,
'We are the Sultans, we are the Sultans of Swing.'

Summer Of '69

Words & Music by Bryan Adams & Jim Vallance

Strumming style:

Play detached, constant down-strums, accenting the first and fourth strum in each bar.

1. I got my first real six-string, bought it at the five and dime.

Played it 'til my fin-gers bled, was the sum-mer of six-ty nine.

Me and some guys from school had a band and we tried real hard.
(Verses 2 & 3 see block lyrics)

Jim-my quit and Jo-dy got mar-ried. I should-a known we'd

Bridge

Man,__ we were kill - in' time,__ we were young and rest - less, we need-ed to__ un-wind. I guess noth-in' can last__ for - ev - er, for - ev- er,_____ no!

D.S. al Coda

✟ *Coda*

Repeat ad lib. to fade

six - ty nine.____ Back in the sum-mer of

Verse 2:
Ain't no use complainin' when you got a job to do,
Spent my evenin's down at the drive-in, and that's when I met you.

Bridge:
Standin' on your mama's porch, you told me that you'd wait forever,
Oh, and when you held my hand, I knew that it was now or never.
Those were the best days of my life.

Verse 3:
And now the times are changin', look at everything that's come and gone,
Sometimes when I play that old six-string I think about you, wonder what went wrong.

Bridge:
Standin' on your mama's porch, you told me it'd last forever,
Oh, and when you held my hand, I knew that it was now or never.
Those were the best days of my life.

Teenage Kicks

Words & Music by John O'Neill

Strumming style:

Intro

Verse

1, 3. Are teen-age dreams so hard to beat_ ev-'ry time she walks_
2, 4. I'm gon-na call her on the tel-e-phone, have her ov-er 'cause I'm

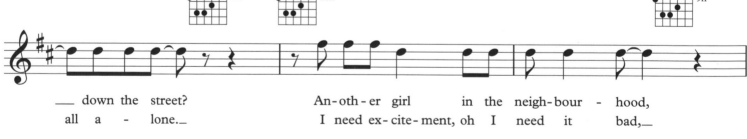

___ down the street? An-oth-er girl in the neigh-bour-hood,
all a-lone.___ I need ex-cite-ment, oh I need it bad,_

Chorus

wish she was mine, she looks so good. I wan-na hold her, wan-na
and it's the best I've ev-er had._

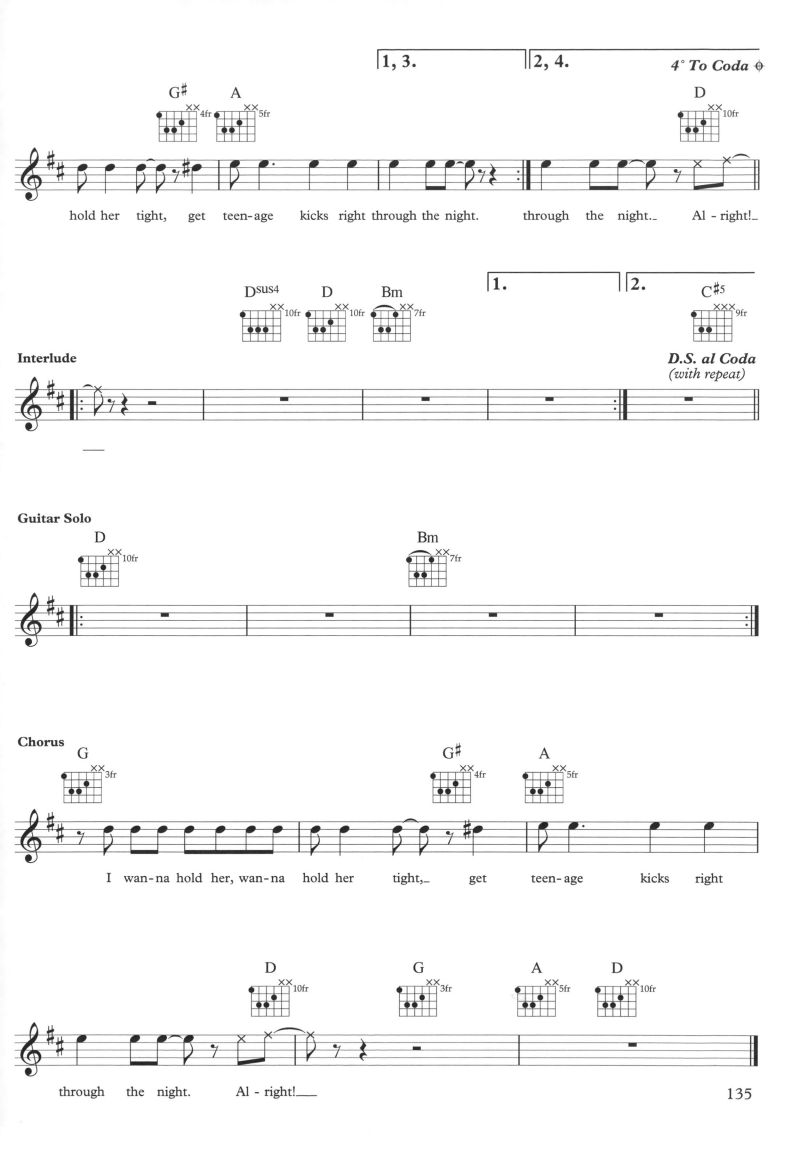

Supersonic

Words & Music by Noel Gallagher

He lives un - der a wa - ter - fall,___ no - bo - dy can see him, no-

- bo - dy can ev - er hear him call, no - bo - dy can ev - er hear him

Guitar Solo

call.

Ah,_____ ah._____ 2. You need to

D.S. al Coda

✛ *Coda*

call, No - bo - dy can ev - er hear him

Guitar Solo

Repeat to fade

138 call.

Use Somebody

Words & Music by Caleb Followill, Nathan Followill, Jared Followill & Matthew Followill

Chorus

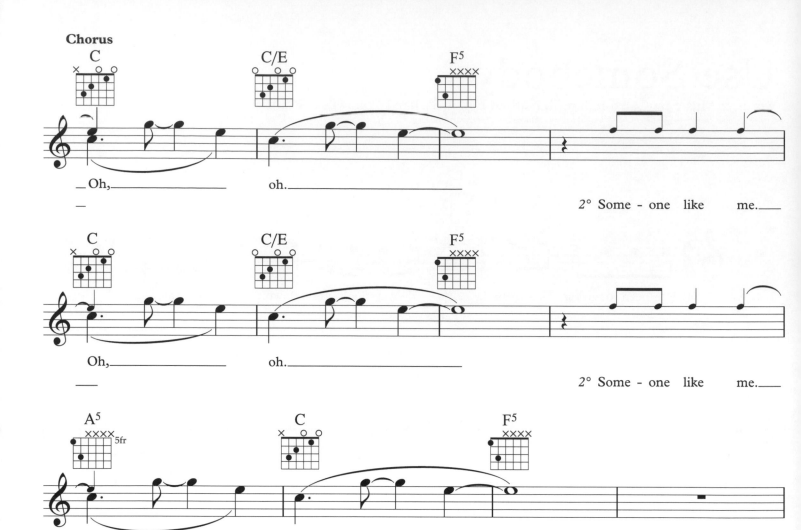

Oh,_____ oh._____

— *2° Some - one like me.___*

Oh,_____ oh._____

___ *2° Some - one like me.___*

Oh,_____ oh._____

___ Some- bo - dy.

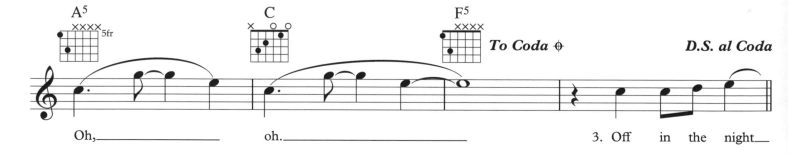

Oh,_____ oh._____

3. Off in the night___

I'm wait-ing. I'm wait-ing. I'm wait-ing. I'm

140 wait - ing. I'm wait - ing. I'm wait - ing. I'm wait - ing.

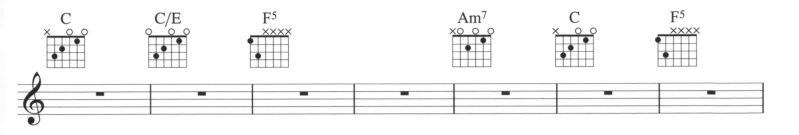

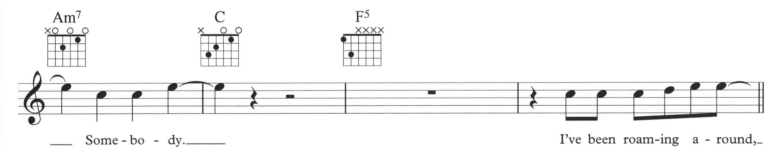

Some-one like you.___ Some - bo - dy.___

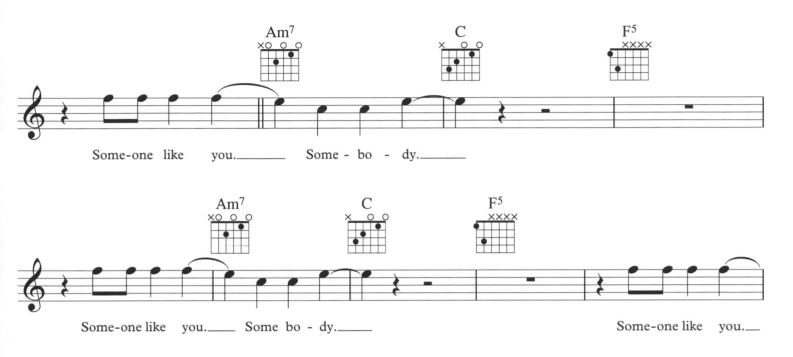

Some-one like you.___ Some bo - dy.___ Some-one like you.___

___ Some - bo - dy.___ I've been roam-ing a - round,___

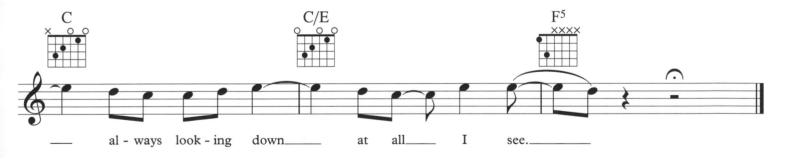

___ al - ways look - ing down___ at all___ I see.___

Verse 2:
Someone like you and all you know and how you speak,
Countless lovers, undercover of the street.
You know that I could use somebody,
You know that I could use somebody.

Verse 3:
Off in the night while you live it up, I'm off to sleep,
Waging wars to shake the poet and the beat.
I hope it's gonna make you notice,
I hope it's gonna make you notice.

Whiskey In The Jar

Traditional

Arranged by Phil Lynott, Brian Downey & Eric Bell

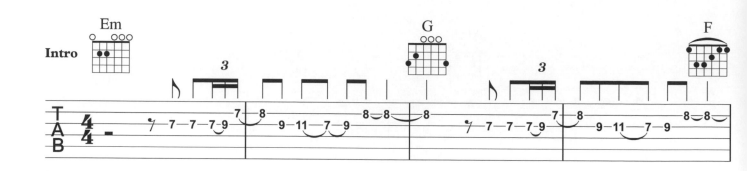

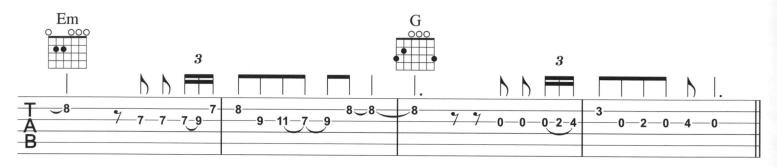

1. As

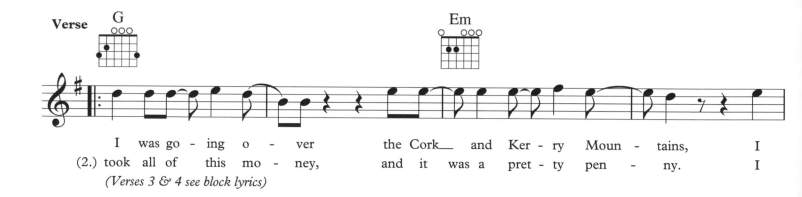

I was go - ing o - ver the Cork and Ker - ry Moun - tains, I
(2.) took all of this mo - ney, and it was a pret - ty pen - ny. I
(Verses 3 & 4 see block lyrics)

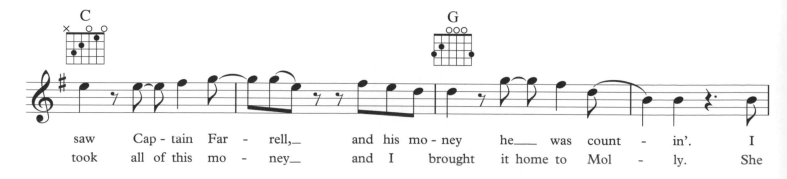

saw Cap - tain Far - rell, and his mo - ney he was count - in'. I
took all of this mo - ney and I brought it home to Mol - ly. She

first pro-duced my pis - tol,   and then___ pro-duced my ra - pier.   I said,___
swore that_ she'd love   me,   nev-er___ would she___ leave___ me.   For the dev-

'Stand or___ de - liv - er   or the de - vil   he__ may take__ ya.'   Mush-a-
- il   take that wo - man,   for you know she   treat_ me ea - sy.   }

Chorus

- ray dum - a - do dum - a - da.   Whack for   my   Dad - dy - o - ah.

(Play intro riff)

Whack for my Dad - dy-o - ah.   There's___whis - key in the jar___ oh.

1-4.

4° To Coda

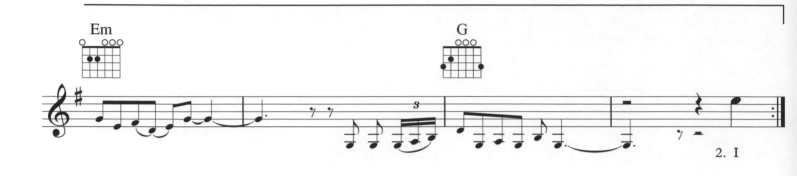

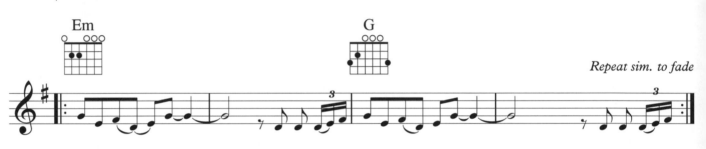

Verse 3
Being drunk and weary
I went to Molly's chamber,
Taking my money with me.
And I never knew the danger,
For 'bout six or maybe seven,
In walked Captain Farrell.
I jumped up, fired off my pistols,
And I shot him with both barrels.

Verse 4
Now, some men like a-fishin',
And some men like a-fowlin',
And some men like to hear
The cannonball a-roarin'.
Me, I like sleepin',
'Specially in my Molly's chamber.
But here I am in prison.
Here I am with a ball and chain, yeah.

Yellow

Words & Music by Guy Berryman, Chris Martin, Jon Buckland & Will Champion

Strumming style:

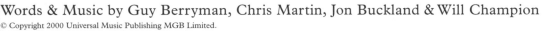

Capo: Fret 2

and it was all____ yel-low.
and it was all____ yel-low.

Chorus

Your skin,_____ oh yeah, your skin and bones____

____ turn____ in_____ to some thing beau-ti- ful.

{ And you____ know_____
{ And you____ know_____

____ you know I love you so,_____
—— for you I'd bleed my-self dry.

you know I love you so.____
For you I'd bleed my-self

dry.

1. **2.**

It's

Interlude

true_____ look how they shine_ for you,_____

look how they shine_ for you,_____ look how they shine_ for,

look how they shine_ for you,_____

look how they shine_ for you,_____ look how they_ shine.

Outro

Look at the stars, look how they shine for_____

___ you and all the things that you_____ do.__

147

You Really Got Me

Words & Music by Ray Davies

1. Girl   you real - ly got me go - ing,   you got me
2. 3. See   don't ev - er set me free,____ I al - ways

so I don't know what I'm do - in'.____
wan - na be by your side.

Yeah,_____ }
Girl,_____ }
you real - ly got me now,   you got me

so I can't sleep at night.____

You Shook Me All Night Long

Words & Music by Angus Young, Malcolm Young & Brian Johnson

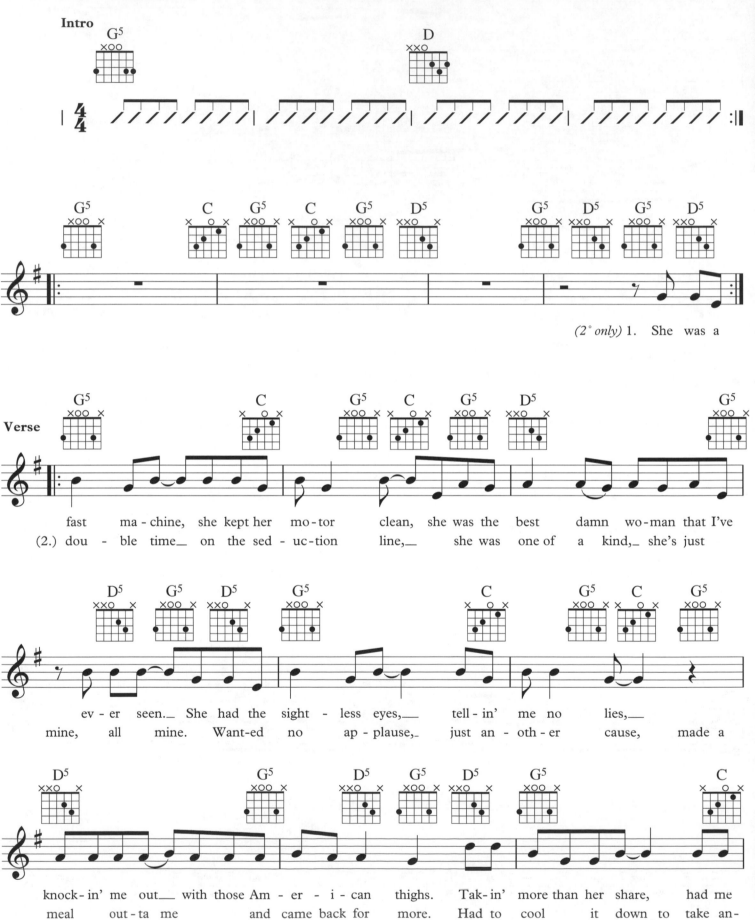

Intro

Verse

fast ma-chine, she kept her mo-tor clean, she was the best damn wo-man that I've
(2.) dou-ble time__ on the sed-uc-tion line,__ she was one of a kind,__ she's just

ev-er seen.__ She had the sight-less eyes,__ tell-in' me no lies,__
mine, all mine. Want-ed no ap-plause,__ just an-oth-er cause, made a

knock-in' me out__ with those Am-er-i-can thighs. Tak-in' more than her share, had me
meal out-ta me and came back for more. Had to cool it down to take an-

(2° only) 1. She was a

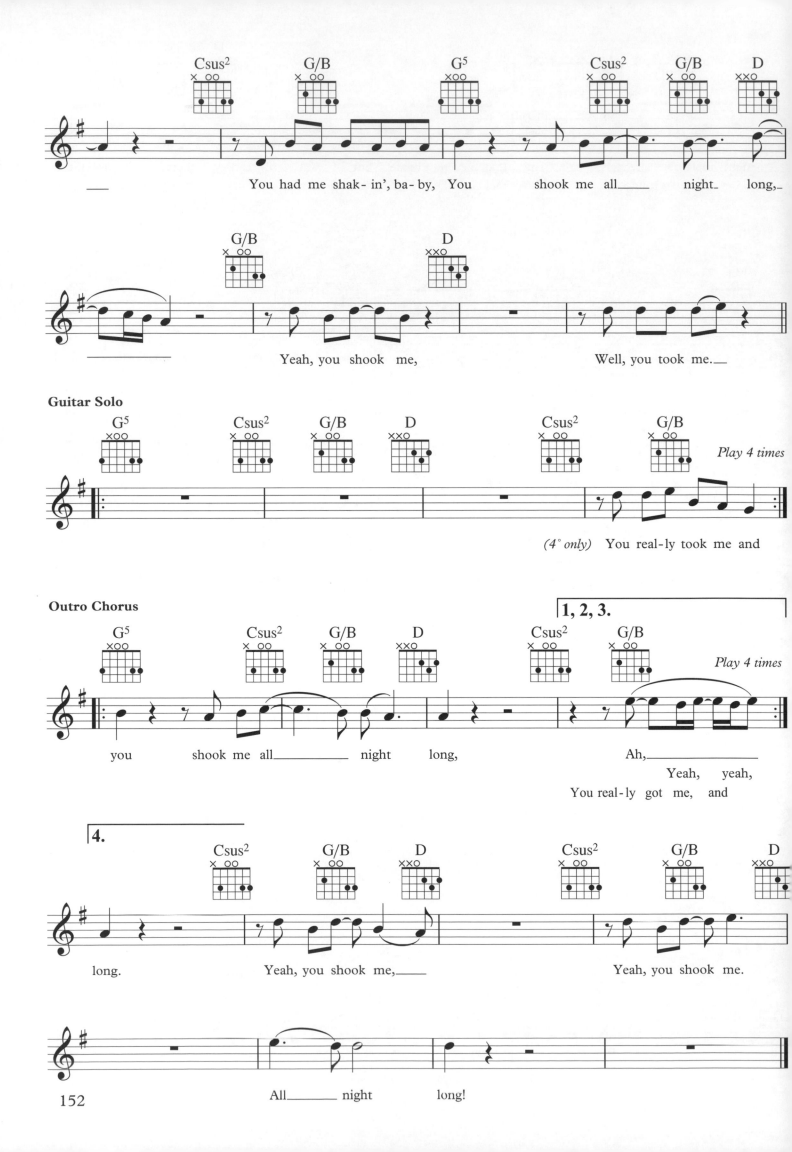

You had me shak-in', ba-by, You shook me all night long,

You shook me, Well, you took me.

Guitar Solo

Play 4 times

(4° only) You real-ly took me and

Outro Chorus

1, 2, 3.

Play 4 times

you shook me all night long, Ah, Yeah, yeah,

You real-ly got me, and

4.

long. Yeah, you shook me, Yeah, you shook me.

All night long!

Ziggy Stardust

Words & Music by David Bowie

Intro riff:

Zombie

Words & Music by Dolores O'Riordan

Strumming style:

it's not me, it's not my fa - mi - ly.
old__ theme since__ nine - teen- six- teen.
In your head,__ in your head__ they are fight-

- ing with their tanks and their bombs and their bombs and their guns. In your head,__

Chorus

__ in your head,__ they are cry - ing._____ In your head,_____ in your
(2° dy - ing._____)

head,_____ zom - bie, zom - bie, zom - bie,__ hey,__ hey.__ What's in your

head,_____ in your head,_____ zom - bie, zom - bie, zom - bie?__